i

Published by
I Heard That Magazine
Ocala, Florida

Dirty World

The Story of Sweet Willy Jones

By Ace O'Rielly

Dedication

I dedicate this book to Earnest Martin Sr.
Special Dedication to my mom Rosa L Martin
and my baby Brenda Young for inspiring me to publish
"Dirty World"

TABLE OF CONTENTS

INTRODUCTION

Some babies seem to come into the world as social beings -- outgoing and quick to smile at familiar faces, while other infants are more subdued. Could simple genetics account for the differences? Child development begins well before a child is born, and each newborn infant is uniquely him or her self, right from the start. Genetic makeup must surely be responsible for some inherent variances in the temperament and sociability of young babies, but as they grow and develop, parental and other family influences are sure to help shape children and impact their social growth and development.

Chapter 1

Meet Your New Daddy

Parents are the keys to intellectual development for almost all children in the care and education they provide and arrange. Many research studies underscore the links between parental involvement and young children's intelligence. Your child's intelligence is being shaped, challenged, and expressed every day by experiences with people, objects, and events — especially when he or she is an active participant. These experiences are the raw ingredients of intelligence.

I figured like this a long time ago; don't nobody care or go give me a damn thing. The only way you get anything in this dirty world, you got to take it out of another man's mouth.

Every day as kid I would come home from school to the scent of sex in the air and the sight of another white man coming out my mom's bedroom, stepping over my little brother, who would be playing on the floor by himself, then strolling their honky ass pass me saying, "What's up, darkie?", laughing.

The same thoughts always would be going through my head as I watched them honkies walk pass me—"If I was big enough to put my foot up this cracker's tail I would in a heartbeat."   But after so many times the crap became normal, you know—routine!

In my little messed up southern town in South Carolina there wasn't no jobs available for a well known whore like Mom except working on her back as a cum bucket for the white boys down at that dirty Cotton Mill.   All the Black boys at that stanky mill didn't want anything to do with her anymo, so she would turn tricks with the white boys to keep the lights on.   Can you imagine, potna?   You a kid coming home everyday seeing a different white man coming out your mom bedroom all the time, looking down at you like you and that slut in there ain't nothing!"   Can you imagine what that does to a kid head, kinfolk?   How mad, how hard that makes him?

1

That's why I dropped out of school at the start of my junior high year. I couldn't take being the trick son of the school anymo, and it didn't help when I broke this big kid jaw in the cafeteria with a chair for calling my Mom out of her name. To cap the situation off, Mom didn't even bother coming up to the school to get me back in because she was too strung out on her back to take time out to check on me. I guess it didn't matter no how, since she had boned the principal of my school a couple of times in our house. Matter of fact, he was one the honkies I wished I was big enough to put my foot up his ass.

It seemed like stuff got crazy fast in our small town. Work at the Mill was slowing down, and those white dudes' wives were getting hip on Mom game, taking money out their kitchen aprons. You see, when money is flowing good everything's cool. Everybody gets their cut, and life is great. But when stuff git tight, then folks want to fight over every little crumb. So it became time for Mom to relocate or suffer a terrible fate.

Mom packed up me and li'l bro and fled to Minnesota. Man, the twin cities was beautiful in the summer time, but in winter it was cold as Rudolph the Red Nose balls, kinfolk. But they also became a perfect spot for Mom to blend in. She settle back into her perfected trade with no problem at all (except for one). Back in our small town she was a free agent, but in Minnesota she had to be associated by affiliation with a pimp. It wasn't any free market selling trim there for Mom. Minnesota was unionized, and she had to pay dues to trick on the 'ho stroll, fa sho, kinfolk.

I'll never forget the first time meeting Daddy, Mom's pimp. This black as midnight looking dude walked into our apartment with a long white coat covered in some type of animal skin crap--mink, fur, or something... I didn't know. He had on a white hat with the same crap covering it and shoes to match covered in the same stuff. I'm sitting on the couch thinking to myself , "What the hell is this?", and the

2

first thing out Mom mouth was, "Kids, this is your new Daddy."

Dude came over to me talking about "What's up, li'l punk? How old you be?" I just looked up at the cat like he was out his freaking mind and said, "I ain't no li'l punk, and I'm old enough, mutha!" Mom came running over so fast and slapped the hell out me, told me I bet' not ever talk to Daddy like that again in my got damn life.

Daddy looked down at me and laughed. I could hear him mumbling, "That li'l punk there gone be something. I can see that in him right from the jump."

One night while Mom was out on the track, Daddy came to the apartment with one of his other tricks, a white girl name Cloudy. Dude didn't even knock... he used a key and came right in. I didn't know who it was so I grabbed a butcher knife and swung blindly round the corner on them. Daddy caught my arm in mid air, laughing talking about, "Come here li'l punk. You got some big balls on you, don't you?"

He told me to go get my li'l brother and for both of us to sit our ass on the couch. Daddy told us that Mom had got busted in a drug raid and wouldn't be coming home for a minute. He told us that Cloudy was one of his main off track whores who would be looking out for us until Mom got out the joint. He said Mom was going to have to pull at least two pennies minimum. I'm thinking to myself, "What the hell is 'two pennies'?" And what the hell my li'l brother go do without Mom? But then I slapped myself back to reality. I have been watching out for him all his life anyway, so no big deal... we'll be ok. Daddy told us Cloudy was our new Momma. He also said he wanted me to ride with him sometimes in order to show me some things about hustling. I had to start earning some money in order to replace what he will be missing from Mom's hustle. He also said it was something about me he dug.

You see, growing up with a mother like Mom made me desensitized emotionally to everything. I had done all my crying a long time ago when I was a few years younger. Now everything is just another day that, "Nobody gives a damn about you in this dirty world, kinfolk."

First night out with Daddy was actually pretty cool. He started out by showing me the other side of the game. We drove by the police station, parked, and then he started naming the police officers by name as each exited or entered the precinct. Daddy told me first thing you need to know is who the law is and what each of their individual tendencies are. He taught me that police officers are pattern mantic; they do the same thing every night on the same schedule, you can set your hustle clock by who's on, which one you can turn out, and basically they weren't nothing but tricks with a gun with enough power to mess up your hustle. Their minds still needed something physically or materially to satisfy whatever Jones they had. I ain't kidding, I didn't understand what the hell Daddy was talking about but I did understand one thing--everybody had a "get paid" hustle.

Daddy took me to the track (or 'ho stroll, as he liked to call it). He said, "Boy, don't look at the 'hoes, look at what you can't see in the shadows." I ain't joking, I couldn't see a damn thing! Daddy said, "Boy, open your eyes and read players brail. See that cat over there in that crème Eldorado watching those two tricks? He's their Daddy, li'l punk. See them Cats over there? Those cats over there are the ones who are messing up the game. They sell drugs to our ladies, turning them into base heads, thereby depreciating the quality of businessmen like myself's product. Now look over there. That's Mr. Undercover Yondi Come."

I asked Daddy, "What's Mr. Undercover Yondi Come?"

He started laughing, saying, "Mr. Yondi Come was the undercover police and when you hear somebody holla

4

'yonder they come', li'l punk, get yo ass to running, because here come the police to bust everybody ass!"

Lastly, Daddy pointed out to me the "gold fishes". Goldfishes is what Daddy called cats that pay street 'hoes for sexual favors. He said the whole game is about product, demand, and supply. Long as those gold fishes crème demands that sex, it's his job to keep supplying it. Then he messed my head up again. He told me to look back over at the "clocker's"! He said, "See them jerks over there, li'l punk? Anytime those cats get anywhere near my girls, let me show you what I got fa they ass." Daddy reached under his seat and pulled out the biggest, blackest gun I had ever seen in my life. He gave the gun to me and said, "'Li'l punk, take this heat and go over there, point this at both them jerks and tell them get the hell up out yo spot. If they don't move like Flash Gordon fa ya, trigger and blast off at them jokers feet, and watch they ass get to dancing like James Brown sliding cross the stage."

Daddy placed the gun in my hand. I jump out his ride, ran across the street and did as told me. You should have seen them jokers haul ass when I put up the strap. And the crazy part about the whole deal was, I wasn't shook... not one bit! In fact, it was like releasing a whole lot of pent up anger. Now I wasn't the li'l weak kid who had to take crap until I grow up. That piece in my hand put me on another level, on a grown up tip, kinfolk.

When I got back to the car, Daddy called me a li'l punk with big balls. The way he said I handle them clocker's was "straight eighty", whatever the hell that meant. Daddy told me a drug dealer was the worst thing to ever happen to the track game. They were the reason why my mother ended up in the joint. He told me that night when Mom got busted by the cops, a bust had gone down in the spot where I just had run them clocker's up off. Mom was on her stroll when one of them dope dealers ran by her and

5

jabbed a baggy full of heroin in her pocket book. When the cops rounded everyone on the track up, including the 'hoes, they found the smack on Mom, and the rest of the story was where it was then. Daddy also said Mom getting touched hurt his business, since she was his real money getter ever since he put her online. Since she's been on lock down he's had a hard time replacing her crème.

Talking about some cold stuff—listening to a dude tell you he ain't making money no more like he should because your momma stuff ain't on the track no mo! That was messed up, what he said, but all in the game, I guess.

Two years passed like water, it seem like to me. Daddy had taught me a lot about money getting and reading folks. Hell, the education I got with Daddy was better than going to school, and I was clocking more money than the teachers at those chump schools anyway, kinfolk. I had a pretty cool job if you ask me. All I had to do was collect money from Daddy girls off the track. He didn't like it when the girls carried a lot of cash on them ever since the new dope game was pushing in on the trim stroll, which brought with it a lot of heat and destruction that effected families, communities and your faith. You could say whatever you wanted to about Daddy, but at least his whores was in church every Sunday morning... back row. Hell, the pastor and deacons wasn't tripping because half them Cats was customers also, ya dig?

I was the type of kid who didn't talk or get attached to anybody—much less grown folks. But Daddy had become real cool with me. I still didn't trust or respect him. I just learned what he was willing to teach. I would be riding with him, just listening, watching everything as he put me up on game, showing me how the system worked. One of my favorite things to do with Daddy was taking his sheep (women) shopping at the Mall of America. It was crazy, seeing this midnight black brother dressed like a peacock and these multi-color fine booty females and a li'l kid like me tagging behind through the mall talking loud and having fun. Daddy bought his whores anything they wanted that was on sale, and he logged in his li'l blue book how much money it cost, notating also in the book a tax percentage charge behind it. Occasionally he would look down at me saying, "These 'hoes got to pay taxes on everything I spend with interest, li'l punk. Nobody gets nothing for free. A good heart will leave yo ass with a broke down Eldo dog on the curve in a snow storm... or worst, li'l punk, dead."

One of the best days of my life even to this day was when Mom got out the joint. Daddy, myself, and four of his other girls went to pick her up. When mom came walking out from behind that wall it was the only time in my life I actually felt something in my heart tingle. But I still showed no emotion. Mom was looking good as hell! Better then that, she was looking healthy and fine. Daddy looked at me and said, "See, li'l punk. Now that's what a vacation do for a 'ho." Then he turned to his girls in the car and said, "I should send all you 'hoes on vacation to that spa tricks.", laughing.

When mom got into the car she was shocked to see me. All the time she had been locked up Daddy didn't let me or my brother talk to or go to see her. He said, "Men ain't supposed to visit the joint to see a woman, especially if she ain't making him no money in there." To me that was some cold stuff he spit out his mouth, but that was Daddy. I guess he didn't get to be the head peacock in charge by having a heart for his 'hoes.

Mom yelled so loud at Daddy for bringing me, it shocked the hell out of me and the girls in the car. She said, "Why in the Sam hell you got my boy here around these whores?"

Daddy raised his back hand to slap mom, but the look on her face was like somebody caught his hand in mid air telling him he better not put a hand on her. Daddy, shocked by the expression on mom face, looked in the back seat at his other girls and said, "Damn! You see, tricks, this is what the joint do to a 'ho, being around a bunch of other caged 'hoes make you brave." Then he gave up that messed up laugh of his, like what mom did in front his girls didn't shake his black ass.

During that long drive back to Twins I sat in back staring out the window quietly. My body seemed so numb, emotionally detached from the sounds of the 'hoes chirping around me, and my mind blank, not thinking about anything... just staring out the window at the different color leafs on the trees as we flossed by.

Ever so often I would hear mom asking me, "You okay, baby?" I would just look at her, shake my head yes, but I could see mom sensing how cold and heartless her baby boy had become. When I look back now. I see that was the first time my Mom every really looked at me with concern because I had become cold and emotionless.

When we got back to the apartment, Mom and Daddy went into the bedroom. I'm standing there thinking to myself "She didn't even take a second to say hello to li'l bro before she was back to her old tricks again. Her bedroom door shut, I grabbed my li'l bro to take him to go get something to eat. I didn't want him to hear Mom and Daddy in there getting it on, but before I could open the front door I heard my Mom yelling, "M F, I'm not tricking no more for you or anybody! That part of my life is over! It's all about raising my boys now."

Daddy must have hauled off and slapped Mom so hard and loud my li'l brother screamed. I could hear Mom falling, knocking over the night stand and lamp. My blood got so cold. I ran down to Daddy car, broke his driver side window out, opened the door and grabbed his gun from under the seat. I ran back up to the apartment, hid my li'l bro in the hallway closet, and bust the bedroom door open where I saw Daddy standing over mom about to strike her again.

Daddy looked at me and said, "What you gone do with that, li'l nigga? Oh, so you a man now, li'l nigga? Pulling that trigger, putting a cap in a grown man, boy, is a lot different from scarring a couple dope dealers off the trim stroll, li'l punk!"

I didn't say a word. I just stared at him coldly with my finger on the trigger. Mom jumped up screaming "Don't do it, baby! Don't do it, baby!" But the more she screamed 'don't do it' the bolder Daddy got, talking that smack.

"This li'l nigga ain't gone trigger no fool. After I take that gun from him, I'm going to kick his li'l tail and yours, 'ho. Then I'm going to sell yo li'l brother to a couple of pedophile punk boys on my John's list, baby."

Soon as he said that about my li'l brother, I shot his ass in the leg. That jerk screamed like a "girl on Halloween". I started laughing coldly while mom was screaming, "Baby stop! What have you done, baby? Daddy was looking up at me in shock, and I'm looking at him like 'forget this dude'.

Then he said the wrong thing again. He said he had been screwing my li'l brother all this time. Before he could attempt his crazy laugh after blowing that stuff out his mouth, I triggered his ass dead in the head, then went over and spit on that jerk's stinking, smelly, defecating body.

Chapter 2

Detention School

I have heard thousands of life stories and have observed that most have maddeningly similar themes. Recounted are early years that are often wrought with child abuse - sexual, physical, emotional and neglect. Growing up in dangerous neighborhoods burdened with poverty, preteen memories filled with tales of sexual encounters, drug use, violence and gangs. The teen years and beyond are laden with more of the same as well as the fathering of children and juvenile incarceration.

by Marisa Mauro, Psy.D.

For killing Daddy I had to do four years in reform school where I got a real taste of reality. Hell, it seemed like all my young life had been preparing me for that place. It's funny now, but when I hear these young rappers today talking all bad, I be imagining if some of them really lived the words they rap.

During that long van ride to the reform facility there was three other cats along with me—a couple of brothers, a white boy, and a Puerto Rican kid. During that ride it seemed like I stared out the van window all the way there with my mind running a hundred miles per minute, flashing back through earlier events in my life that led up to that point. In my subconscious state of mind I still kept tabs on what was going on around me in the van. I could hear the two brothers talking about what they were going to do when they touch ground on the yard of the juvie. One brother talking about how he was going to beat somebody down right off the bat, the other had a cousin inside he was going to hook up with. The white boy was sitting all the way up front behind the driver staring into the driver's rear view mirror the whole time, looking scared as hell. The Puerto Rican kid was sitting in back of him with the same expression on his face.

Mr. "Bad Ass" brother turned to me and asked what was I on the long haul for (whatever the hell that meant). Without saying a word, I turned to him, gave him a look he didn't particular care for, then turned my attention back to staring out the window. I could hear him say to the other brother, "Oh, we got us a Mr. Bad Ass. We'll see how bad he is when we get inside the box (cell)." Then he turned his attention to messing with the white boy and Puerto Rican kid. The one brother was messing real hard with the Puerto Rican kid, talking about he had some pretty hair and joking about how nice he bet it would look if he grew it long when they get inside. The Puerto Rican kid didn't say anything. He just sat there with that scared look on his mug like the white boy.

Whoever said incarceration rehabilitates is out'a their damn mind. Being sent to juvie is some messed up stuff. It only prepares a kid for that other level of the game, I'm telling you. From the second I got off the van in the breeze way to the entrance of the processing building, my mind clicked into animal mode. Throughout the long drive up to that point I had been programming my mind to click into "f... it" mode. Soon as my feet touched concrete, my mind shifted into survival mode, meaning I wasn't going to take no crap off no one, no matter who they was or how big. If I was cold hearted before, now I had become Eskimo nose cold, me against whatever/whoever.

Going through the welcome process was messed up, too. I think they degrade a kid on purpose, just to mess with his head. But my head had been messed with a long time ago, so that crap didn't faze me not one bit, when they paraded our naked asses through the hallway like a 'ho being chose in a whore house. But the white boy and Puerto Rican kid, they asses was crying like little tricksters, for real. It didn't help any with those other two kids from the van walking in back of them talking crap bout how much nicer their asses would look with a tan, occasionally looking back at me smiling. The only thing that was running through my mind as I looked expressionless back at them dudes was, one or both of these two kids is gone be the first ones I mess up for real, and they don't even know it yet."

After being processed they split us up. They placed me in a box with this tall muscular cat name Sam from St. Paul. Sam was a light skinned brother close to six feet tall at fifteen years old. It was like somebody had said put this li'l kid in with the baddest mutha on the block, because that's just what they did. When I walked into the box and seen that thick, over grown kid, first thing ran through my mind was, "Hell, let the games begin." Dude stared me up and down, and I stared back at him like "Let's do this crap, potna. You may whip my ass, but you gone know you been in a fight, potna." One thing I had learned from watching dogs, even the littlest Chihuahua—you may stomp your foot and he take off running, but when you try to stare him down eye to eye, he's gone show teeth and growl at you, not back down. So there me and this cat was up there eye balling each other for what seemed like two days until he said, "Forget you dude. Take the top bunk!" I didn't say jack, I just threw my stuff down, crawled up and put my conscious mind in relax mode, but kept my subconscious mind or one eye on that big young'n.

****

My first night being locked behind that white door in that small cube was insane. You could hear young boys crying, some having sex, while others were hollering gang calls. I just laid there emotionless. Actually, I was thinking about my little brother until the noise around me was slowly drowned out by my thoughts of Derek. Over and over, replaying, hearing those words Daddy spit out his mouth that put me in this spot, wondering was it true. Did he violate my little brother, that black, no good, dead mutha? With those thoughts running through my mind I couldn't sleep. Occasionally Sam would say, "Yo, kid, be yo behind still, making all that noise tossing and turning!" I wouldn't say anything in response. I just laid there in my own world. Matter of fact, from the moment I got into the cube with Sam I never said one word to him... no small talk, nothing, 'cause I really didn't care about who he was or where he came from. Far as I was concerned he was just another cat I would have to step into at some point. So why befriend any of them?

You be surprised how fast the days go by when you're locked up. Sam and I had gotten really cool. We would be on the yard peeping cats 'ho card. Sam had his own little hustle going on. He was the cat everyone came to for permission to execute a bank on someone (beat someone up). Anytime someone got banked, sexed up or sliced, they had to pay Sam before it went down. Talking about some crazy crap, how can a cat have a hustle getting paid off saying yes or no to letting a cat get got? That crap still amazes me to this day, but that's the way it was in that dirty world.

I remember lying on my bunk one day chilling out. Sam was out on the yard doing what he do, when both of those cats from the van came walking pass our cube. Now, one rule Sam had was no one can come into our crib without asking permission. But I guess they hadn't got the memo. They seen me laying on the bunk and came into the crib without an invite trying to step to me. I'll never forget that crazy situation. One of them told me I was gone drop down and blow him right then and there. Before I could leap out my bunk fast enough Sam snatched up one of them niggas from the back while I was in mid air like Hector Macho Camacho with my trusted rope I made from tying pillow case clippings together. I wrapped it around the other kid neck and proceed to strangle the hell out his ass. Harder and harder I tightened. All I was thinking about was Daddy violating my little brother like these two slobs wanted to do me. Out of nowhere Sam pulled me off him yelling at me, "I

13

didn't give you permission to kill, li'l nigga! Back yo ass off!"

You should have seen them niggas haul ass out the cube like the tricks they was! After that, I would see those niggas in the yard... those 'hoes wouldn't even look my way. I had heard a couple of days before they pulled that bullcrap on the Puerto Rican and white kid. I guess they luck ran out when they got to me. But it wasn't over yet. I went to Sam for permission to do something to both those jerks—not for what they tried to do to me, but in my mind for what Daddy said he did to my little brother. Plus, when you share the same space with someone you try to kill unsuccessfully, it's only a matter of time before they try to get you back. So one or two of us had to go, and I made my mind up it was going to be both them cats, ASAP.

I didn't have any money or nothing to trade but I made Sam a promise. When we got out I would take care of him. I didn't know how but I would. That big dude looked at me and said for some reason he knew I would because of my character, so he gave me the green light to handle my business, but he couldn't help me any further than that. I was on my own.

Thanks to Sam I had one of the best jobs at the time in juvie. I worked in the cafeteria and infirmary. When I think back now that's probably how that dude got that big, because everyone who worked in those areas was recommended by his ass and was always sliding him a little something extra in the yard. Since I knew chow times, I put my plan into action. I got some rat poison and prepared a special dish for them cats on soup and crackers night. I mixed two healthy bowls of special rat-ton-soup up and placed it on the side for my two friends. When they came through the line, I had it planned with the white kid they had violated to step to both of them when they get to me in the chow line and start a commotion so I could do a slight of hand, placing the special bowls of rat-ton-soup on those assholes' tray. It worked to perfection. Those asses ate that crap up and about two to three minutes after they had guzzled that crap down they went into convulsions... both them niggas shaking like Don Knots. I stood behind the chow line emotionless just looking at them asses fade away into eternal sleep. Nobody moved to help them, either. Even the guards moved like they had a thumb stuck up their asses, which made me a little curious. But I just said, "HELL WITH THEM!"

After that drama things got real easy for me in that joint. Sam had gotten released early and went back to St. Paul, while I finished rolling out my time in peace. Well, except for a few words that was circulating around the joint about the cousin of one of them dead niggas I canceled was planning a get me back, but it never came.

Chapter 3

Free at Last!

There are already more than <u>two million</u> men and women incarcerated in America's jails and prisons. When all of the people incarcerated are combined with all of those on probation or parole, the U.S. correctional population exceeds <u>seven million</u> people. That means <u>one in every 32 U.S. adult residents is currently under correctional supervision!</u> We all arrive at periods in our life when we sit down and reflect on the path we have chosen in life—often regretting certain choices and missed opportunities. First of all (and this is important) - You cannot turn the clock back. It is scientifically impossible.

On the day of my release I recall walking out that place switching my mind from animal lock down mode back to free world normal. Mom and my little brother was there to pick me up, and for some reason all I was thinking was these muthas supply you a free ride here but you're on your own getting back where you came from when they cut ya loose.

It was good seeing my little brother. He had gotten tall and, damn, did that boy talk a lot now. Mom had kept her word the whole time I was on lock down by not tricking anymore, and I could see her and Derek had really bonded while I was away. Mom said she thought it was time for us to make a fresh start. She was just waiting for me to get out so we could move the family to Detroit, Michigan. After about a year, like the Beverly Hillbillies, we packed up everything we had in a Mayflower truck and headed to the unknowns of the Motor City for a fresh new start.

When we arrived in Detroit, Mom promised things was going to be different. She said she was no longer going back to tricking. In prison she got what was back then equivalent to a GED and learned how to sew, making uniforms. Our first night in Detroit Mom said she was going out for a few to see what the night life was like in the city. She again promised that she wasn't going to turn tricks, just see what was happening.

16

When Mom came back to the apartment later that night she was with this tall, slim older cat around sixty years old, he looked like to me. Me and little brother looked at each other at the same time and said "DAMN! Here we go again." It was like Mom had read our minds and said "Hold up boys... It's not what you're thinking. This is William, he's a Supervisor at the Ford motor car Plant. I met him tonight at a bar. He bought me a few drinks, and then offered to give me a ride home." Hell, I breathed a sigh of relief so big I farted. My little brother busted out laughing, along with William, while Mom stood there shaking her head in embarrassment.

William turned out to be cool as hell. Since he worked as a janitor at Ford headquarters in Dearborn, he used his connects to get Mom a job working at one of their assembly plants on the line. Then he moved us out that raggedy ass, rat infested basement apartment we had to take when we arrived in town into a house across the street. I started feeling like "Leave It to Beaver'. William even got me a job at a car detail shop on Gratiot Avenue (Eastside Detroit), and my little brother finally went back to school, bringing some type of normalcy to our lives.

The detail shop for me would turn out to be a blessing or a curse—still can't figure out which one it was. But the joint opened my eyes to the under belly hustle of the Motor City. I mean, cats from all walks of life came through the shop to get their rides touched up. Back then it was all about pimp'n 'hoes, slamming Brougham doors in the Motor City and getting your pinky ring lean on, daddy. I would just watch cats like Daddy taught me. Dudes would come up to me on a regular, talking 'bout "What's kicking, li'l nigga? Why you don't bust it up with us (talk with them) like the other workers?" I still wouldn't say anything to them. I would just nod my head and keep working, but the corner of my eyes and ears were wide open. I was learning who was who in the street game. There was the "want-to-be pimps".

17

These dudes weren't very hard to peep out... all around the world they had the same *flash* and *talk*, but no 'hoes anyone had ever seen walking the track for them.

Then there was the drug dealers. It was only two differences between them and the pimps to me. One was the amount of money they flashed. Drug dealers loved for other cats to know how much money they're holding. I use to enjoy listening to these cats brag about how much money they make and how many gals they got. But in reality, *they* was some of the biggest tricks in the city. *Drug dealers spent more money paying for snatch than the gold fishes.* The second difference was the pimps took money from 'hoes and the drug dealers paid to have 'hoes on their jockey team.

Then there was the undercover narc. They use to come through the shop to get the rides they probably confiscated in drug raids in another City washed... small talking, and hanging around trying to listen and see who's who. Last, there was the auto Worker. Every hustler called them *marks* or *guppies* because everyone ate off these suckas. Pimps sold them tail, drug dealers sold them a taste, and what the police and court system didn't get, maybe their ol' ladies and landlords got back at home. Every day was a real circus up in that spot, with real life clowns.

Back at the cut after my work day, I use to lay back and register in my mind all the information it had absorbed throughout the day at the shop. A couple things kept coming up. All these hustlers are getting the majority of their paper off a single source, the auto workers. Without them this city would be like my home town when the cotton mill closed. Everyone ate off GM, Ford and Chrysler. The other thing that was running through my mind was how much I hated drug dealers. I didn't feel the same about the pimps because a woman is going to get in where she fit in to get paid and selling her tail is a guaranteed survival commodity that she has. Besides, selling snatch don't destroy communities and families, kinfolk.

Chapter 4

Along Comes Tracy

If we are honest with ourselves and others, we all have made wrong choices. There have been times in our lives when we went in the "wrong" direction. There was a struggle as a result of this. How we handled our failure spoke volumes about our character as a person. So, what do we do when we are faced with the aftermath of making a wrong choice?

One day up at the shop this fine as hell black chick came through. Baby girl was built like Marilyn Monroe, dark skinned, reddish blonde streaked hair with hazel brown eyes, and pushing a brand spanking new Cadillac Deville with the chromed out angel on the hood guiding her way. I'm telling you, this was the first time in a long time something shook me and got my attention. Dude, this chick came walking in the shop on some Coffee Brown tips. Even the pimps backed up, and the dope boys put their money away. You could've heard a mouse steal cheese in there, kinfolk. She stepped to the counter, looked around, then told my Boss she wanted me to clean her ride. I ain't go lie, I was standing there looking at her in amaze, because 'hoes, to me, always rolled in the back seat of the El dog, or on the 'ho stroll dress like this chick. I certainly never seen one that made hustlers backup. My boss threw me her keys and said, "Drop what you doing, li'l nigga, and take care of that." Now this crap here was crazy. Ol' girl looked at my Boss and said, "Is that how you talk to your workers, nigga?"

Everyone in the shop was like, "Damn!"

My Boss put his head down and said "No, Ma'am." Then she made him *apologize* to me.

The whole time I was cleaning her ride I could sense someone watching me, but I kept my head down doing my job... still keeping tabs on my personal space in case someone ventured too close. When I completed cleaning her ride I brought the keys back in to my boss and gave them

19

to him. Ol' girl told him to give them back to me and that I would no longer be working there anymore. My boss and the other hustlers mouths fell so wide open you could've pissed in them and put the fire out in the their stomachs, because they was hot. She looked at me and asked can I drive. I just nodded 'yes'. Then she told me to bring her car up, open the passenger side rear door for her, and that I was her new driver. I did as she said, but before I turned away I looked over at the drug dealers and gave a dirty look to them I hadn't felt in a long time because I knew my life was about to take a u-turn with this chick. I wouldn't have to be around them anymore suppressing what I really wanted to do to all of them. I hated drug dealers.

Ol' girl told me her name—Tracy. We drove to her high rise condo in Southfield off Greenfield Avenue and Ambassador Drive. The whole time I'm driving we didn't say a word to one another except the few times when she gave me directions to where she wanted to turn. When I look back now that crap was crazy. It was like I was asking her questions in my head and she was answering them but no words was spoken. We had a natural flow to our auras.

Riding up the elevator to her Condo all kinds of crap was going through my head, but I maintained my usual calmness like the coolness to the other side of a married couple's pillow. When we stepped inside her Condo my mouth wanted to drop, but you know me—show no emotion or reaction. Her crib was laid out and on point. I still remember it like yesterday, how I stood there thinking to myself, "This trick must have that holy grill between her legs, kinfolk, cause she sho nuff getting paid off it, and ain't no 'ho I ever knew lived like this! Hell, no *pimp* I ever knew, either. She took me to the first bedroom on the right and said "This is your room! You will be living here, and don't worry about clothes or anything... it will be provided for you." Now I'm really shakin'. I'm standing there like— "Hold up, lady! Up until now I have been rolling with you, but it stops here." I told her I couldn't live there. I had a little brother who needed me to be home for him. She looked at me and said, "I know you have a little brother name Derek, and your Mom work at Ford, right?"

I told her again, "Hold up, lady. Who are you, and how you know what you know about me?" She told me she knew people, and it's a small world. That's all I needed to know, and if I didn't want to roll with her program I could take my black behind back to the shop! I stood there for a few seconds, trying to ice grill her down. But she showed no fear. Finally I said, "Forget it. What I got to lose? I'm rolling with you for at least a minute, Ma'am."

I was thinking to myself, "Don't roll out or step to her about how she knew so much about me, because I was curious about a black trick with as much class as she was shown." I figured my best chance of learning what was going down would be from the inside, close to this trick. That's why I choose to roll with her on whatever program she was putting down at the time.

Tracy opened my eyes to another side of the game from a female business woman perspective. She was making mad loot off of her professional and political male clients. She had something I had never seen up until then. She had male 'hoes, and the crazy thing about that was her male 'hoes made more money than the females! Tracy business was top shelf, exclusive. Her workers didn't hit no track or hoe stroll. It was by appointment only, cash only up front before the date. That's where I came in. My new job was to pick up the money from these professional tricks before the 'hoes was sent out. No money was to change hands between the johns and 'hoes. That way if anything went down, no one could get accused of prostitution and it made it easier on the 'hoes. This way they didn't have to haggle with the johns over price or worry about getting Tracy money stolen.

One of the first things Tracy taught me was how to dress for the job. All the dope boys shopped at places down town Detroit, like City Slickers or the side walk shops in the hood off one of the 'mile' roads. The pimps had their threads custom made. But me—Tracy took my ass to JC Penny's. She said that professional men bought their suits off the rack from what was at the time high end department stores. She couldn't have me going to their offices dressed in all those colors looking like the NBC peacock picking her money up. So, shopping down town Detroit at City Slickers for rags was out the question. Her clients were high end, low profile and commanded a lot of respect and privacy. So I got all decked out in my new plain navy blue suit, white shirt, black tie, Braham shoes, and started my new job. To drive, she bought me a brand new green Ford Granada with an eight track player; it was clean but not flashy.

My first pickup was a trip from the moment Tracy told me where it was. I had to go up to Ford Headquarters in Dearborn off Michigan Ave to pickup money from one of their Executives for a date that she had set up. In the back of my mind I was thinking, "Damn, I hope I don't run into William" and sure enough soon as I step foot into the building, who in the Sam hell you think I ran into? William... mopping the entrance floor, slangin' that mop and greeting folks just like a real house nigga. He asked me why was I up there! I told him I was there to pickup this gal I had met for a lunch date. He asked what girl was it, because not many black women worked up there at the time, and he knew all the ones that did. As much respect as I had for William, my business was my own, and explaining to him wasn't on my list to do, so I told him I had to go, and to tell Mom and Derek I would be by to see them that upcoming weekend. After I walked away from William I put on the fake badge Tracy had made up for me to wear and walked straight to the elevator, up to the third floor, to the john's office like she told me to. When I got up to dudes office, his secretary (without saying a word to me) reached in the top

22

middle drawer of her desk, pulled out a envelope, and handed it to me. Without saying a word back to her I slid the envelope into the inside top pocket of my suit jacket and hit the slopes (left the office).

For the next two months it felt like taking a pacifier out a baby's mouth collecting money. Tracy's hustle was a gold mine without having to break one brick. Plus, her top shelf 'hoes was almost flawless in their looks. That alone kept the clients coming back.

Visiting all three of the big three headquarters collecting money became routine. Even to this day I couldn't tell you what the clients' faces look like, but I know them some horny little devils! Man, if their wives only knew! I used to laugh to myself thinking, "If these assholes could write snatch off on their taxes as a donation, every charity they donate to wouldn't have to beg regular folks like me for bread."

And don't let it be executives from other countries flying in for a meeting... it would turn into Christmas for Tracy and her gang of 'hoes, especially if it was them horny little Asian dudes. I swear, them cats love them some white gals with blonde hair. Tracy would jack the price up on them if she knew they horny little asses was on the menu. They got the special double up dollar/yen conversion rate for them won-ton soup eating Japs.

Chapter 5

Surprise, Surprise!

> *In debating sexual orientation, much is unknown. According to Charles Darwin, "...we do not even in the least know the final cause of sexuality. The whole subject is hidden in darkness." Although the APA currently states that sexual orientation is not a choice, rather that "...it emerges from most people in early adolescence with no prior sexual experience, social theorists argue that an individual's upbringing can directly influence this sexual orientation." Also tied in with many of these debates is the morality of homosexuality.*

A couple of months passed fast and I hadn't visited or called my family. Working with Tracy turned out to be a full time job, seven days a week. It was not like I couldn't visit—I just wanted to separate myself from them until I had learned what I had gotten myself into. When I figured there was no threat to them in this business, I figure it was time to pay them a visit.

It was a cold Saturday morning I went rolling up to Mom's house. When I walked in something didn't feel right to me. I called out for Mom, but no one answered. So I called out for Derek, and could hear footsteps upstairs hitting the floor and moving fast. So I called out again, "Derek, is that you?"

He yelled back, "Yeah, it's me! What are you doing here this early, RJ?"

"I came to visit you, nigga! Where is Mom?"

"She stayed all night at Williams last night. Why?"

I started walking up the steps with that uneasy feeling. Derek was sounding too weird for me. He hadn't seen or heard from me in months and his first reaction when I show up is to question why I'm there? Something wasn't right with that scene. Each step I took up the steps, I heard the footsteps scrambling fast around upstairs. So I speeded up to the top only catch a short li'l nigga I never seen before panicking trying to hide. I looked at Derek and asked what was going on up there, and who was that nigga?

Surprise, Surprise!

Derek ass was up there telling me to calm down, it's not what I think it is. I told him to tell me what I'm thinking is not true, then. He couldn't. He couldn't look me in my eyes and tell me him and that cat wasn't up there screwing. It took everything in my power to keep from killing him and that nigga, but all I kept thinking was Daddy did this. Daddy's dead ass turned my brother into a fag. I yelled at the li'l gay nigga, ordering him to get his ass out my Mom's house in two seconds or else he will be getting something other than a dick up his ass. I sat on the top step thinking, "All those nights I tossed and turned in bed back in the juvie, my life's worst nightmare has come true. Derek is gay! My li'l brother is a fag, and I can't do a damn thing about it! It is what it is. Over and over in my mind I was seeing all the gay boys Tracy be sending out on dates with some of those twisted executives, …all the homo stuff in juvie, all that crap was messing with my head. But you know what? It is what it is. If his ass want to be a cock sucker then let him. Forget that fag! I don't want nothing to do with his gay ass. I couldn't accept that crap back in juvie and can't except that crap to this day!

I never did tell Mom about that morning, and we never did talk about Derek being gay. I still believe to this day she knew, but it was a subject she would always shy away from whenever someone mentioned anything about homos. Derek and my relationship suffered also. I didn't want anything to do with him, brother or no brother, even though in back of my mind I still blamed Daddy for being the primary reason for Derek turning out the way he still is to this day. I think because of Derek, my relationship with Tracy grew stronger. She became like the sister I never had, and I was starting to do something I felt I never could—trust someone. She encouraged me to go back to school at night to further my book education. I needed to learn how to run a business the right way since I had the street smarts. But in order to take it to that other level, I had to learn how to think on that other level. She always said, "Boy, you have to start thinking like them corporate white pimps. Pimp them with the ink pen, baby." There was something still bugging the hell out of me about Tracy that we never talked about. But I felt it was time...

One night we were having dinner at one of her favorite Jamaican restaurants on Jefferson Ave when I finally had to ask that burning question that had been haunting me. How did she know so much about me and my family? Tracy put down her fork and stared me straight in my eyes with a look that would freeze water. "I guess you have earned an answer to that question", she said.

"When I was sixteen years old, I was sent to live with my aunt and uncle in Memphis, Tennessee. My uncle was a damn drunk, and my aunt was a weak excuse for a woman. My uncle use to try to get in my panties almost every night when his ass came in drunk, and my aunt, that trick turned her head like she was deaf when I would scream for her. So I ran away to Chicago. When I got off that greyhound bus in Chicago I didn't have any money or a place to stay. All I knew was I had to get away from my aunts place. Well, I met this guy name Donald. He was a tall, dark as midnight, handsome brother round about my age. We hooked up, he gave me a place to chill, and soon after, of course, we became lovers. At first everything was cool. He had a little hustle running numbers, and when one of his customers had a hit, they would break him off a little something extra. That's when he would buy me something beautiful. I was really starting to think he loved me because I sho nuff was falling for his black ass. Oh, how I loved that big black nigga! I would have done anything for him, and eventually I would. One night he came running into the apartment panicking, frantically yelling, 'We need to get out of here fast before they get here!' I was like 'Who?' He kept saying 'Baby, hurry up. Please! We got to go now.' I grabbed what he allowed me to, and we took off to Minnesota.

Surprise, Surprise!

"When we got there it was beautiful, summertime and all. I really thought we was going to make a new start there until what little money we had ran out. That's when one night he turns to me, his woman, and asked me to trick with these drug dealers who had been digging on me. He said it would be a onetime thing only. It would earn us enough money to make it until he found a new hustle. That one time turned into many times.

"Then that Negro started to bring other girls in... younger girls. He started to dress and talk different. Soon the guy I had fell in love with was selling my ass to whatever john came along with two dollars! I sold my ass on them cold streets of Minnesota for six months, until I had saved up enough money on the side to get me a bus ticket to here.

"When I went out to work that last night it was the last time I seen or heard from that black nigga. I still had a few friends back there who I kept in touch with, so I always kept tabs on what that black mutha was up to. Then, after all those years, the call I had been waiting on came through. My friend told me Donald was dead."

I drop my fork in cold shock and looked up at Tracy. "Donald?" I questioned in my mind.

"Yes, Donald, baby. I think you call him 'Daddy'! You killed the man I loved, who first turned me out. I just couldn't believe he was taken out by a kid", she said. "I was curious about the kid who killed my man, and did some research on you and your family. I followed you throughout the trial and your time in juvie hall. Do you remember a kid in there name 'Sam'? Why, sure you do! He was your bunk mate, if I recall... right?

I just sit there in disbelief staring hard at Tracy with a look that could kill again.

"Sam was my friend's nephew. I made sure he was taken care of by having a few of the guards Johnson sucked by my connects in Minnesota. In turn, they made sure Sam was taken care of and Sam made sure you was taken care of.

It all started coming back to me. Nobody in the joint ever trip with me except those two niggas from the van. I didn't even have a problem with the turn keys. Even when Sam got out, the rest of my time was spent like I was chilling in Holiday Inn or something. Tracy went on to tell me that her friend was the one who planted the idea in my mom head to move to Detroit when I got out. She also said that William was a friend of a friend, a really nice older guy that she thought would be good for my mother. He didn't know anything about her or her business. He was just put in the right position at the right time to meet mom, and the rest was where it was then.

While Tracy was telling me all this I just sat there with no expression on my face—emotionless, thinking how someone could just manipulate your whole life... and for what purpose? I told Tracy I wanted to ask one more question. She nodded her head in approval!

What the heck did she want from me and my family? She told me that since I killed Daddy, something she had wanted to do for a long time, I earned her respect and deserved a new start in life. At that point and time, her answer was good enough for me, since me and my family was doing a hell of a lot better now than any other time in our lives.

Without saying or asking her another question, I picked up my fork and continued to eat like the question was never asked. Tracy looked at me and said, "Boy, I see so much of me in you, and it scares me." Then she picked up her fork and continued to eat.

The next morning when I got up for breakfast, Tracy was already at the table going through her appointment books. We said good morning to each other like we always did... no words, just that look of acknowledgment to one another. Tracy told me it was time I franchise off. She said it was only a matter of time before some of her high powered clients would do something stupid like send the law at her.

You see, one of the biggest problems with men of power—those cats talk too much to 'hoes after getting laid, and say some crap about their business or company that they shouldn't. Then, when they regain their senses, they want to back track and do some house cleaning and everyone becomes expendable. Since the only folks whoever saw my face was the secretaries, I was cool. But Tracy, she felt she was going to be in some deep crap soon, so I had to branch out from her hustle into another before she caught a case, or worse, ended up dead.

Tracy told me she had a whole new business plan. She said we where no longer going to sell trim to high profile men. Instead, sell dick to their wives. The only secrets them high class 'hoes tell is beauty secrets and they're the ones who have all the money, and don't have to account for nothing long as they stay out their husbands way. "We were now into the selling Johnson business to trophy wives," Tracy said, with a serious look on her face.

I moved out of Tracy's high-rise into my own condo in Birmingham, Michigan. Tracy had an interior decorator lay my pad out with some tricked out crap at the time... modern art deco type crap. She even got me a new Ford Granada, black with the fifth wheel on the back. But the manner in which I dressed stayed the same—JC Penny's suit, shoes, tie and never flashy. I thought I was cold! Tracy was off the chain when it came time to finding new clients for her new service. It wasn't hard at all. This was a lady who did her research for real. She had been laying the ground work out for this new venture for some time. I figured it out because her first clients was the wives of the high profile executives she had been servicing all this time. Suddenly it all came back to me... all those times I dropped her off at those day spas, women social retreats, and charity functions! She had been networking, gathering clients up from those horny as hell executive trophy wives, and that accounting book she always worked on at the breakfast table was a listing of them horny little socialites.

Chapter 6

On to Phase 2

> *Intention is the most important of all mental events, because it gives direction to the mind, determining whether we engage with virtuous, non-virtuous, or neutral objects. Just as iron is powerlessly drawn to a magnet, our minds are powerlessly drawn to the object of our intentions.*

Tracy came over to my apartment on a Saturday morning. Since she had a key she came right in, into *my bedroom*, and sat on the end of my bed. She told me she needed to speak with me about my role in the new service. I'm a tell you, what she said next really messed me up, fa real! Tracy told me I was going to be servicing her new clients. Without saying a word I rose up in bed, pulled the covers back, got up, went to the restroom to take my morning piss, came back and sat next to her on the end of the bed. I looked her straight in eyes, wiped my hand across my face and said, "Tracy! I've never been with a woman before. She looked at me, smiled and said that's why you're perfect, baby."

I didn't trip on what she told me I had to do because I knew nobody ever do anything for you just because they like you. It's never something for nothing. If you wait them out long enough their true motives for looking out for you will be revealed. So when she broke it down to me it was actually a relief, because now I knew what she wanted from me.

Before Tracy could put me into service we just had that one little problem, or should I say, one *big* problem that had to be overcome. I never had been with a gal or woman before. Don't get me wrong, I knew about doing. I'd been around it all my life, but actually doing it *myself*, my mind wasn't ever there. The first thing Tracy told me was sex brought a lot of emotional baggage, and I had to separate the *pleasure* side of it from *business*.

While Tracy was talking it seemed like I didn't hear a damn thing she was saying after the part about separating the pleasure from the business. I started thinking about my Mom. All those years growing up screwing one cat after another like it wasn't anything. Was it pleasure or was it business for her? That's a question to this day that I would love to ask her, but the past is best left in the past. Then I felt Tracy touch me on my shoulder. "Hey... are you here with me?"... snapping me out of the deep thought I was in. Then she stood up, told me to go take a shower and in two hours come back over to her condo and come directly back to her bedroom.

After two hours I did as Tracy told me. When I got to her condo I strolled back to her bedroom and knocked on her door. She told me to come in. This was the first time I had ever stepped foot in her bedroom, so when I opened the door and seen candles lit, incense burning, and smooth jazz playing, I said to myself, "What's going down in here?" Tracy was lying in the bed looking sexy as hell in a way I never looked at her before. All this time she had become like a sister, a mentor, to me. But now I was experiencing something in my pants I hadn't before when looking at her. My Johnson swelled up rock hard, and my brain was sending signals throughout my body that had me a little weak in the knees from the sight of her. Tracy was lying on her bed in a red lace see through teddy. Her breasts was perfect. I could see the imprint of her dark round prefect breast, long nipples firmly bulging through. Her stomach was perfectly flat and the site of the thickness of her shaved snatch bulging out the bottom of that teddy made the blood in my veins flow like warm water down to my Johnson. My Johnson grew like Stretch Armstrong. It was a sight unbelievable to me that my Johnson could get that big and thick without having to take a leak.

Tracy told me that I had to make love to her. She told me that she would guide me through every movement so I would know what to and not to do when trying to please the type of women I would be dating. I told her I couldn't make love to her. Making love to her would be like screwing my sister. She said that's exactly why I *had* to screw her. I had to learn how not to get attached emotionally to any of the women I would be servicing, that's why I was going to start with her.

"Screw it," I said to myself. "She's right. For one thing, she ain't my sister... And it's about business, not pleasure." I guess that's why all this time she had been letting me get so attached to her, so she could break me down for this moment. That was some cold crap she pulled. But it was cool, since in the back of my mind I knew me and her emotionally was cut from the same cloth.

When Tracy finally felt I was ready to represent her in the field, she sat me up with this older chick, around fifty years old. She arranged for our meeting to be at the Ambassador Hotel, downtown Detroit. When I walked into the suite and seen this old white chick already in the bed, under sheets, I really wanted to laugh out loud, but I kept that crap professional. "Ain't this a switch?" I said to myself. My first ass on the job, and Tracy sat me up with this old hag here. But knowing Tracy, that crap there was some type of test. I just knew it. One of the things Tracy taught me was that *snatch* is *snatch*, no matter what the woman you are going to screw look like. The face of all snatch look the same, so you screw it the same... only difference is the mind and body type of the woman you are about to screw. You have to treat every woman different in a special way before you penetrate her flesh. You have to penetrate her mind first, so look past what she look like and attack her mind first. Getting her off mentally first saves a lot of time and money because she'll get off quicker and fantasize about you later, whereby establishing a return customer who also will tell her social club members about our service. Remembering what Tracy said, I quickly dismissed the visual and concentrated on the task and technique at hand. I ain't go lie, I turned that ol' gal out so much she tried to give me an extra tip, but I wouldn't take it. For all I knew that ol' hag could've been undercover, since I knew Tracy already had gotten paid. So the compliment was good enough for me.

It didn't take long for word to get around among them uppity tricks about this young stud who knew how to do it to their mind and body. Tracy's new business venture had paid off just like she planned. I had them uppity executive wives lining up for an afternoon Johnson cap. I never knew how much Tracy was charging them horny tricks, but I knew she was getting paid royally by my take. It was business, so I wasn't tripping. Tracy had put a lot into setting this thing up, so to me she deserved whatever her take was.

Tracy only set up one date a month for me. She said too much sex would burn me out and devalue the quality of the service. By letting me turn one of them trophy 'hoes out a month also ran the price of my services up. Actually, it started a bidding war among them, and I would only be sent out to service the highest biding socialite. All the sex I watched Tracy sell to them executive sex feins at the Big Three couldn't compare to the amount of money that was being generated from freaking just one of their wives. Those heffas had an open check book to spend on whatever the hell they wanted to long as they stayed out their husbands business and way.

After about six months of what I look back now and call boot camp, Tracy came back over to my condo again and sat at the end of my bed. This time before she said anything I raised up, pulled the sheets back, got up, went took my morning piss, came back and sat next to her on the end of the bed. She looked at me and said, "You're ready now. I didn't say a word, I just nodded my head. No matter what it was she had planned I was rolling with it. I had grown to respect and trust her decision. She had never led me wrong up till that point.

While Tracy was laying out her new business plan to me, my house phone rang. It was my Mom. She told me I had to get over there quick! Something had happened to Derek. I told Tracy I had to bounce out quick. I got dressed and made it over to Mom's so fast it seemed like two seconds hadn't went by. Even though I hadn't talked to Derek since I caught him with that sissy boy, I still was concerned about my li'l brother.

When I got there, Mom said Derek was upstairs going crazy, throwing stuff around and yelling at her like he was on something. I quickly ran up the stairs only to find my li'l brother ass bone necked in his bedroom closet with the door open writing on the walls with a pen knife. His eyes were glossy and the room smelled like I be damn! I told him in a calm tone to give the knife to me. When he looked up and seen it was me, he started crying. He dropped the knife, jumped up hugged me so tight I thought I was gonna lose consciousness. He kept repeating my name over and over again. I pulled him off me, ripped the sheet off his bed, wrapped it around him and sat him down on the end of the bed to examine his eyes like a doctor would. Derek had got hold of some bad dope. I'll never forget how I felt then. I wanted to kill every one of those drug dealers on the streets of Detroit. "Those muthas!" I kept saying to myself. Give my brother some bad junk, right? I got up from Derek, closed his bedroom door and for the next three days I stayed locked up in that funky ass room with him while he was Jonesing, trying to dry out. Finally after three days when he came down. I asked him where he got that crap from. He told me from a drug dealer who I remember from coming up to the detail shop when I worked there. The messed up thing about it was, this cat knew me from there, knew I worked for Tracy now, and to top it all off he had learned Derek was my brother. Now, me and this cat never had a beef because I didn't talk or get involved with crap when I was working up at the shop. So why this cat would want to hurt my li'l brother? Whatever, it wasn't going to be too healthy for his future.

Back at my condo I was pacing back and forth across the floor thinking, "Why did that dude mess with my brother? If he had a problem with me he should've addressed it with me, not my family."

In the middle of my thought the phone rang. It was Tracy. She told me I was going to have a special visit in two days. I told her I didn't think my head was ready for work. She told me that she knew what had went down, and she needed my head clear before we could continue with business. So I had to get this issue resolved before we could move on. She also told me that I couldn't be involved in nothing. That's why this visitor has been called in to handle whatever I was planning. Now, in my mind I'm thinking, "How in the hell do she know what's going on? I haven't said anything to her about my family issue." But then again, it was Tracy. What didn't she know about me?

A couple days went by when I heard this heavy handed knock on my door, sounding like a mutha was trying to knock my stuff down. I grab my Saturday night special, firmly tucked it in my right hand behind my thigh and yelled back "Who is it?"

"It's me li'l nigga! Open the door!"

"WHAT? SAM???!" I couldn't believe it. It was my dog Sam, from Minnesota. Now, that nigga was big at fifteen back in juvie, but now he was a monster, fa real... built like Tony Atlas, muscles everywhere (and this was before steroids).

35

Soon as he stepped into my place, first thing that big nigga said was, "I see I got to keep yo li'l ass out of trouble again, huh li'l nigga?"

I stood there with a puzzled look on my face. I asked him how he knew where to find me, and what was he doing here. When I asked him, he said all he knew was he got a letter with my info in it and a boat load of cash to come to Detroit to handle an issue. The letter also stated that I would be instructing him when he got here. I didn't say anything to Sam, but it didn't take a rocket scientist to figure out who was behind him showing up at my cut—Tracy.

Sam and I wasted no time plotting out our mark. The tripped out thing about drug dealers are they have the same routine and tendencies that they follow everyday like clockwork. Every other day the dude would bring at least one of his rides up to the detail shop for cleaning at the same time, rain, sleet or snow. This fool had to shine even if it was for six minutes. After the detail shop, he would ride through checking on a few of his traps. Then by his stash house, one of his trick's crib, and last to the strip club to launder some of his day's take. We followed that nigga for about a week, and in doing so, learned a lot about his hustle and operation, which was a pretty good one. That's why it puzzled me even more why would he want to mess with a nigga like me. I ain't had crap nor was I a threat to him.

Dude had a perfect laundry money hustle going on. He would go to three strip joints a night, spending boat loads of cash on these stripper 'hoes, but there was a catch. Them stripper 'hoes worked for him. Every night after collecting a certain amount of money, dude would go to these stripper clubs and trick with them sack chasing strippers that worked for him. They would take all the money he gave them, turn it in at the end of the night to the club owner (his boy), and he would deposit the money into a business account the next day, cleaning it up. They had to pay taxes on the money when the club filed at the end of the year, but, so what? Long as the IRS git their cut, they don't mess with you, no matter how much you make, long as you don't make a mistake filling those W forms, potna.

My plan for this drug dealing scum was really simple. He needed to taste his own bad junk. Having Sam bust a cap in that fool's head didn't appeal to me, since I only preferred to use a gun if it was a quick situation I had to get up out of. We planned to kidnap his ass after he made his last pickup when he was in route to the first strip club.

We arrived at the strip club about an hour before he normally did, and parked in a spot next to the entrance where he usually park. Just like clockwork, he showed up on time and parked where we expected. When he pulled into the parking spot the driver side of his door was adjacent to the passenger side of ours. When he starts to get out, we planned it where Sam opens his door at the same time. They both stopped quickly before their doors hit. Sam apologized and nodded for him to go first. When he got out his car, Sam got out of ours behind him. As he started to walk forward between the two cars, Sam grabbed him from behind placing a handkerchief dosed in chloroform over his nose and mouth, putting that fool right to sleep. Afterwards we drove him to an abandon building on Michigan Avenue outside of downtown Detroit near Tiger stadium.

When he opened his eyes he found himself foamed and duck taped. We placed foam around his wrist, ankles, and chest before securing him down with duck tape. That way when he was found dead it would look like another nigga overdosed. Leaving tape marks would lead to too many other questions and possibly a short Detroit homicidal investigation. I left his mouth untaped because I needed answers.

"Why did you mess with me by giving my li'l brother that junk?"

Dude started laughing when I asked him, talking about, "You and that trick think y'all smart, right, nigga? Y'all thank y'all got the high price snatch game on lock, right?"

I asked that nigga what the heck was he talking about. Dude said he had been trying to cut in on Tracy actions for a while now. That trick shouldn't be running the high price snatch game. And then my flunky ass come along out of nowhere and she put me right up on the game. So before stepping to Tracy, he thought he'd send a little message to her. But I told the cat he did it at the wrong person expense, and it was too sloppy. My little brother ain't having crap to do with me or Tracy, and now his ass was go get a taste of his own junk.

Before I pumped that nigga up, I couldn't believe it. He was still sitting there about to die, still talking crap. He said Tracy was using me, and that it was only a matter of time before those white executive muthas would want their names erased from her little blue book. And if I was still hanging around her, I would go down too, because they also knew all about her new hustle on their wives.

To me, at the time I didn't give a care about none of that crap he spit out his mouth. With every hustle there's risk. You just have to choose the one you are willing to deal with.

I proceeded to inject with two dirty needles a load and a half of his own junk into his arm, then stepped back and watched that son of a bitch wiggle like Tina Turner, same way I watched those two chumps back in juvie kiss the baby bye-bye. After he went drifting into eternal sleep, we dumped his stankin' body on the Eastside on Seven Mile Road, in a pile of old rubber tires for anybody who was concerned to find. Sam kept all the money he had on him, a little extra thank you from me to him, of course. Afterwards we went back to my Condo.

On to Phase 2

We were chilling out listening to some Barclays on my new eight track deck when Tracy called. Only thing she asked was, "You okay now, baby?" I told her I was straight! Afterwards she said it was time for Sam to leave. He had served his purpose, but now we had to get back to business. So I sat around with him for about another day before sending him back to Minnesota with a small paper bag of money.

Some of the crap Dude was saying before we canceled him still rang out in my head, but I kept dismissing it because in any game of hustling someone is always looking over your shoulder to take your spot, and Tracy spot was no different except she was a female getting that Boys Club money on their turf. I didn't even bother to tell her what that nigga spit out his mouth. Somehow I felt Tracy already knew. That's why she was always one step ahead of them clowns and so helpful with arranging to get at that turkey. I also figure it was her way of sending a message back to whoever he was clicked up with.

When I got over to Tracy's Condo she was in her usual spot at the dining room table sipping on a glass of wine, listening to WJZZ, going over names in her blue book. I sat at the table in my usual spot with my head held down like normal. Without lifting her head she told me that we were no longer servicing those executive wives anymore, and that business in Detroit was getting too tight. For the last six months she told me she had been getting more involved in politics since the Primary Caucus was coming up. Attending different political events in Detroit, flying to DC and other parts of the country to Democratic and Republican Party's events, she managed to make quite a few connects among the wives. I raised my head up slowly and asked her, "Tracy, you want me to screw politicians wives?"

She looked me straight in my eyes and said; "YES! *Snatch* is *snatch*, right?" I nodded my head in agreement, then replied, "Why can't you get some other cat from here?"

Tracy didn't say anything. She closed her book, got up from the table, took a few steps away from the table, then turned back to me with a serious look as to say 'read my mind'... and that I did. Without saying one word, just those brief seconds looking at me before turning back to walk away said it all. She was saying to me she'd invested a lot of interest, time and money in me, so I didn't have an option. I guess we were now in the screwing politician wives business.

Chapter 7

More Than a Woman

How can ignorance bring us suffering? ...The conventional explanation is that because we are not omniscient, we regularly get ourselves into trouble. We do not realize all the consequences of our actions, we do not understand other beings and we do not understand why the world is exactly the way it is. So we often end up in situations where we do not take the best actions. Just reflect for a moment how often we think: "If only I had known this earlier..."

That night after Tracy revealed her new plan to me I must have tossed and turned all night in bed, replaying earlier events in my life... all those times I came home from school to see another white man coming out Mom's bedroom, stepping over my li'l brother, and walking pass me saying, "WHATS UP, LI'L NIGGA?"; all the women I seen sell their trim for Daddy and got nothing but crap in return; and to top it all off, me and Mom serving time locked up like animals behind all those tricks. I've always despised Mom for being the town whore, and now I'm no different from her. It seemed my life so far had come full circle now. I'm a 'ho, getting pimped just like my Mom did herself.

I couldn't sleep and was hungry, so I decided to go get something to eat. Since the only place I knew that was open at three in da morning to get a bite was White Castle on Woodward and Eight Mile Rd., I threw on a pair sweats and my Pony tennis shoes, hesitated for a few seconds in deep thought, remembering one of the things I hated about living in those suburbs was being out late riding Woodward Avenue, especially driving through Birmingham and Troy. Those honky cops loved to screw with a brotha, especially one in a nice ride. Lucky for me, Tracy made sure my papers was right, just in case I had any static from the pigs. Knowing her, the Chief of police was probably in her blue book.

Normally when I go to White Castle I go through the drive through instead of going in standing in that long line, but this particular night I was in no hurry to get back home. When I stepped in the place it was just like I figured—a line of brothas and sustas all dressed up looking like peacocks, straight from the clubs. White Castle was the spot to get a bite after the clubs closed. It was also a dude's last chance to pull a female if he didn't get lucky in the club. But that crap didn't faze me. I just wanted some of them quarter gas burgers to go.

I'm standing in line minding my own business like normal, waiting for my turn at the window, when I see these two young gals staring at me. I'm thinking to myself, "What the hell them 'hoes looking at... my Johnson out or something? All these other cats in here to game on... What the hell they looking at me for?"

After placing my order I went and sat at a table in back to wait on my number to be called. One of the young gals came over and sat in the chair adjacent to mine at the table I was chilling at. She didn't say anything at first. She just looked into my eyes, which was really starting to piss me off. Then she asked, "You're lonely, aren't you?" This gal had the sexist hazel eyes, so warm and deep. I almost fell into a trance looking back into them. Now, I can spot a 'ho from White Castle to the Detroit River, and this gal wasn't a 'ho. But I still rudely responded to her anyway.

"No, I don't want to buy no snatch". I really expected and wanted her to get up and get the hell out my face, but she didn't. Instead she read me like an open book. She started telling me I had trust issues, I spend a lot of time alone, I'm heartless, I'm loyal, and that I wanted to make a change in my life but didn't know how. Now, all that other regular crap she said Phil Donahue could've guessed, but when she said I needed a change in my life... that for some reason struck a chord.

I didn't say anything back. I just looked at her like she was out her mind. But inside I was curious. Her gal friend then called her to come on so they could leave, but before she got up she wrote down her phone number on a napkin and, without saying any last words, slid it to me before walking away. I picked up the napkin, balled it up in my hand and was about to slang it, but for some reason, I didn't. When I got back to my ride I threw it on the passenger side seat. I wasn't about to call no female... just wasn't going to happen in this life time.

Not many things, people, or even Tracy could mess with my head, but that young gal really did. For the next couple of days I was all off track thinking about her, I kept picking up the napkin with her number on it debating with myself if to call or not. Tracy was the closest person to a female friend that I had ever known, but our relationship of late seem to be business only. Plus, Tracy and I never talked about anything personal. We both was too cold hearted to show such weakness.

I never dated a gal my age, or any age, for that matter. All the females I've ever known was track whores, only good for bringing that money off the 'ho stroll, not for conversation. I wouldn't even know what to say to a descent gal. I've never known any, and something inside me was telling me this gal wouldn't be like what I was use to.

It was a snowy Saturday morning when I finally made up my mind to call her. I ran out to my ride in that snow storm, trying to find that napkin I balled up and threw somewhere in it. I must have frozen my ass off before finally finding it between the passenger side seat and the door. You should've seen me out there, freezing my nuts off, shaken like Lucy on crack, trying to dig that sucka out that tight area. After warming up a few minutes and getting my nerve up, I dialed her number.

This old broad answered the phone. I thought it was her mother, but it was her grandmom. I asked for Connie, and got what seemed like forty questions in return—"What you want with my grandbaby? How old are you? You got a job? What yo momma name, boy?", etc. Since I grew up down South I still had the highest respect for old folks. So I politely answered her questions as honest as I cared to be in a respectful way before she gave the phone to Connie. Connie got on the phone apologizing for her grandmom, but I thought it was kind of cool, the way her grandmom act like a guard dog. That showed me a little what type of gal I was about to get involved with.

That first day we talked on the phone for about twelve hours, it seemed like. I never knew a gal could talk as much as she did. Being around Tracy had turned me into pretty much a mind reader. I wasn't use to someone, especially a female, opening up to me, telling everything about them without it pertaining to selling something. Connie gave me the exclusive run down on her life. I don't think she left a damn thing out, either. But for some reason I wasn't bored or tired of hearing her talk. In fact, I enjoyed listening to the sound of her soft, patient voice. It really relaxed my soul.

Connie's world growing up was much different from mine. Although she was sent to live with her grandmom at an early age because her father was in the military, her family was still close. She attended private school at Cranbrook, but she had plans of going to Michigan State and, most of all, she knew where she wanted to go in life. I'm on the other end of the phone thinking to myself, "Damn! A female with future plans that don't revolve around snatch and Johnson… go figure!"

When we got to the part about what I wanted out of life, a deep silence fell over the phone. What I want out of life? I asked myself in my own head that very same thing. Connie had hit me with a question I had never thought about.

I've thought about how to get revenge on cats, how to collect money from 'hoes and johns, how to read tricks like Tracy's mind, how to stimulate them old tricks mind Tracy sat me up with so I wouldn't have to screw them as long, and, most of all, how much I hated living in this Dirty World. That one sided conversation with Connie made me stop focusing on all the things I've become desensitized to and focus on me instead.

Connie and I started hanging out more. We'd go to the Detroit Artist Institute on Woodward Avenue just to sit on the steps and talk. We would frequent Jazz clubs, do movies, all the crap I thought a cat like me didn't like. But most of all, I loved when we would just lay in my bed with our clothes on all night listening to WJZZ and her mouth just a'runnin'.

In my mind I knew what we were starting to build couldn't last... not as long as I'm indebted to Tracy, and she didn't really know what I did for a living. I told her my aunt was wealthy and her husband didn't want me to live with them, so she provides the Condo and car for me to keep me out his head. Did she believe it? Don't know, but she never questioned me. All she would say is, "When you're ready, Richard." Richard... I hadn't heard somebody call me 'Richard' since the judge gave me that time in juvie. Everyone had always called me "Li'l Punk", "Li'l Daddy", or "Sweet Dick Willy". Now that I think about it, my mother really messed my name up, naming me 'Richard Jones'. Maybe she was thinking about screwing then, too. Who knows? But the more Connie called me by my real name, the more I started feeling like a real person, not a nigga or a sex object.

As much as I wanted to, Connie and I would never have sex. I never had much of a sex drive anyway, but I felt if we would have made love, then I would become emotionally attached to her, since we had built so much

45

together outside of the physical. Plus I knew I had some unfinished business, so I did what any cat in my shoes was suppose to do. I looked Connie dead in those beautiful brown hazel eyes and told her we couldn't see each other anymore. She didn't cry or say anything, and that really messed me up. On all those movies she had been taking me to see, them 'hoes broke down like old Chevys when they man told them they were leaving. But Connie looked back into my eyes and told me she had been waiting for that moment.

I'll never forget, as she was getting out my ride, turning back to me and saying, "When you're ready, Richard, I'll be here". It was like she was telling me to go handle my business and she'll be there when my mind is clear. I didn't say anything back. I just drove off into the slushy icy streets, leaving her standing there (I could see her in my rearview mirror) watching me drive off. I guess that's what Tracy was talking about when she said *'catching feelings'* because I was feeling something. But I kept telling myself "Man, it is what it is, and that's all it's gonna be, so keep it moving, R.J."

I drove straight to Southfield to Tracy's condo. I think I needed a reality check. When I got there, of course Tracy was in her usual spot. But this time she raised her head and commented, "So your little puppy love crap is over, I hope! Can we now get back to business, Li'l Daddy?" I didn't know how much I hated Tracy calling me 'Li'l Daddy' until that moment. I kept saying over and over in my head, "I'm not yo 'Li'l Daddy', trick! My name is Richard Jones, and I'm tired of being your 'ho." But I kept that crap to myself.

It was no doubt that being with Connie had an effect on me and the way I saw things now. I was no longer looking at myself as being in debt to Tracy. That freak was just using me, anyway, from the jump. I was starting to believe her calling me "Daddy" has to do with some physiological crap with her experience with the real Daddy. Maybe some reverse mental stuff, I didn't know. But I knew one thing—it was time for me to start thinking about getting out the Johnson slinging business for her.

Back in juvie, I learned a few things from listening to cats talk in the yard. "A thief can spend more time than you thinking about how to break into your home, than you can about how to keep him out". That being understood, I wasn't going to under estimate Tracy's thinking. She put a lot of time into planning and keeping tabs on me, so any plan that I could come up with to get myself out of this situation had to be pre-calculated and executed with patience. She didn't lay out this plan without having some type of failsafe in place just in case I decided I've had enough. I know her. I had to figure that out before I could even begin to strategize an exit. But until then, I went along with the program without any questions, like I've always done.

The Democratic National Convention was gearing up in New York City, and everyone was on Jimmy Carter's Johnson since Tricky Dick (Richard Nixon) and Freeway Ford (Gerald Ford) had screwed things up so bad. Now, Tracy was ready to put her plan and connections into play. All conventions were about anyway was the after party. All the bullcrap speeches them lying politicians make is just to get their party loyalist hype before the after party.

Tracy called me the morning before the starting day of the event to tell me it was time for us to go to work. She had already made flight arrangements for us to fly out of Detroit Metro that night for New York. She also told me to pack up three of my navy blue suits, wing tip shoes, white starched collar shirts and red neck tie. She had got me in as a young interning page for a representative (whose name I can't mention) as a favor for her. I guess she must have had something on him in her blue book for a hookup like that.

47

When we touched down in New York, Tracy had arranged for a limousine to pick us up and take us to our hotel. After we retrieved our luggage out of baggage claim, I seen this big black cat in a tight black penguin suit, white shirt, black tie, and a crazy black hat (looking like a young George Foreman in a Pee Wee Herman suit) holding up a piece of cardboard with Tracy name on it. After we got into the limo, well on our way, Tracy told me that we would be staying in two different hotels, but the buildings are right next to each other, adjacent to the convention location. She said that we would be in town for three days, and all three days I had appointments setup, so she recommend I didn't spend too much time taking in the sites of the city.

When we arrived at our destination, Tracy was dropped off first. She told the driver to take me to my Hotel and make sure I got settled in okay. If I wanted to go anywhere, even if it was just walking, he was to escort me. Now, I'm setting there listening to her bark out these instructions to this cat who I don't know, and I'm wondering if this cat gone be my body guard, chaperon, or Tracy's watch dog over me? But then I tried to justify Tracy's actions as her just not wanting anything to happen to her investment in a strange city. Besides, I knew she had a lot of cheese lined up to get.

After I got settled in my room, I told ol' boy I wanted to take a walk and look around a bit. I actually thought it was pretty cool in a way, having my own personal watch dog, because dude knew the city like the back of his hands.

New York was beautiful, much different from Detroit, and a hell of a whole lot opposite of that little hell hole in South Carolina I was born and drug up in. The buildings were so tall they blocked out the sun. There were people in ever different color speaking in languages that all sounded like Swahili to me. One of the things I wasn't feeling about New York was the people. They all seemed rude and in a hurry. Even the older folks I walked by seemed rude. When I spoke to them, they didn't acknowledge me. They just kept it moving like I was invisible or something. At least down South folks had manners. But those New Yorkers seemed like they had too much on their minds to be neighborly. So I said, "Hell with them!" and continued my site seeing of the Big Apple.

When we arrived back in Detroit the first person I called was Mom to see how her and Derek had been doing. Mom told me that Derek had been trying to get in touch with me for the last couple a days. I asked her what he wanted and was he okay. She told me physically he appeared to be doing okay. He didn't seem like he was on anything since that earlier episode, but he was acting really strange... nervous in a way. I told Mom soon as I get myself together I would be over to talk with him.

My mind was racing a hundred miles a minute thinking all kinds of crazy thoughts about what could be wrong with Derek. I prayed that he hadn't started using again after almost losing his mind messing with that junk before, but I was in no frame of mind to go talk with him until I'd had a nice hot bath to try and boil off the immoral filthiness from my trip.

I sat in the bath tub soaking, over and over in my head trying to think of a way out from under Tracy control. She was smart and cunning. No doubt she had in place a backup plan just in case I decided I wanted to split. If only I could hate her, or she did something to me that turned me against her. Without something like that to ignite me I couldn't get into that vindictive frame of mind to do anything to her.

The business part of our relationship was cool, and Tracy had been nothing but good to me on the personal tip, so I couldn't find any malice in my heart to hurt her. I tried weighing all the pros and cons of my life with Tracy.

Pros: I made good money, I lived good, Mom worked, Derek in school, I have a nice ride and, most of all, I had plenty of money saved up. Cons: just one... I'm no better than what I saw as a kid everyday in South Carolina. I'm a whore, just like my Mom was, and that, to me, outweighed any of the pros. I would rather be broke than to remain what I so despised all my life, and that was my own Momma.

When I got over to Mom house, Derek came running out to hug me. William was there also, but for some reason he wouldn't look up at me when I spoke to him. William and I had always been cool. I had a lot of respect for him for what he did for us, so it puzzled me why he didn't acknowledge me. But I just said, "Hell with it!" to myself, and continue to talk with Derek.

Derek wanted to go out to Belle Isle Park and talk, so we got in my ride, jumped on the Lodge Freeway to Jefferson Avenue, then straight to the park. Before we got to the park, I stopped off at a party store that was before the turn off to the entrance to the park to grab a couple soda pops and chips. I gave Derek some money to go in while I sat out in the car and waited, listening to my new Johnny Guitar Watson eight-track. Then Derek came walking out the store talking with this gay boy that I knew who worked for Tracy. I rose up in my seat. When the fag saw me he was startled so bad he almost dropped the bag he was carrying. He looked at Derek, then back at me, and then took off running so fast that sissy could've caught the Road Runner.

When Derek got in the car he asked me did I know ol' boy. I told him 'No!' Derek then asked me why he reacted like that when he saw me. I told him I didn't know, and to stop asking so many questions. Then I switched the crap up on him and asked him what the hell was he doing talking to a punk boy? Derek wouldn't answer that crap. He just told me to forget it and just drive to the park. I let it go, but I wasn't finished with that question.

Belle Isle Park was jumping. When you drive through, it's always like a car show going through there at two miles per hour bumper to bumper, watching everyone get their pinky finger lean on. Everybody and their momma were out there; pimps, players and pipe layers, shining, getting their mack on, trying to pull them young gals.

I backed into a parking spot, turned down my eitht-track, looked at Derek and said, "Let's talk, nigga!"

Derek looked at me with a frightened look, one that I hadn't seen on my little brother face since that day I killed Daddy rotten ass.

Derek told me he knew how I made my money. He even knew who I worked for. Then he messed my head up. He asked me do *I* know who I work for? I didn't say anything; I just looked at him coldly. Then he yelled at me "DO YOU KNOW WHO YOU WORK FOR, R.J.?" Again I didn't say anything. What my little brother said next took my heart right out of my body. Derek screamed so loud I think the Canadians on the other side of the river heard him. "YOU WORK FOR DADDY *SISTER*, R.J.!"

I was speechless. It was like gravity had taken my head and forced it back into the head rest. I remember repeating over and over to Derek, "Derek, don't mess with me. Derek don't mess with me!" until my eyes closed. But I didn't fall asleep. Instead, I started visualizing Tracy from the first day I saw her up to that bullcrap explanation she gave me when I asked how did she know so much about me and my family.

Derek shook me—"R.J.... R.J., you okay?" I remember Derek telling me something to the effect of when my eyes opened up it was like he was looking into the devil himself eyes. Derek told me the whole story... how Daddy was Tracy big brother, they were from Minnesota, their parents where middle class, both worked for Three M, and they both were spoiled kids growing up.

51

Tracy was the one who got her brother into pimping. She had plenty of gal friends she use to set Daddy up with for fun. One day she got the idea to test him by betting him he couldn't get one of her finest friends to turn a trick for him. Daddy was always charismatic with the chicks, so in no time at all he had her turning more than one trick for him. Having Tracy for his sister only helped his status. Having a fine stallion for a sister like Tracy in his corner to recruit 'hoes for him only solidified him as that dude and increased his reputation around the twin cities.

After Tracy set Daddy up in the game in Minnesota she looked at branching out, so she targeted Detroit because of the automotive industry and all the businesses that supported and benefit from the industry. Tracy was also getting a kick back from Daddy hustle, so when I killed him, the word on the streets was that this little nigga who killed her brother took a lot of money out her pockets, and that she wasn't too happy about that, along with the fact a freaking kid took out her kinfolk.

I asked Derek how he found out about all this crap. He told me the guy I saw him talking to at the store told him. I asked him where he met that nigga, and he told me at a gay party in Highland Park, off McNichols and Woodward Avenue while I was out of town. "That m.f.", I said to myself. "That's why that punk ran when he saw me. He didn't know I knew Derek... or did he?"

A few things still puzzled me with Derek's info. I had to make sure what he was telling me was on the up and up. I asked Derek how the subject came up about Tracy at a gay party. All her workers had been with her for a minute, so why, out of the blue, would one start running their mouth to a total stranger?

What he told me next I really didn't want to hear, but it was what it was. Derek and that sissy had been kicking it way before the weekend I was out of town. Just like a man when his Johnson is in some snatch more than one time and the sex is good, he'll start running his mouth telling everything to a female, even the combination to his safe. And those sissy boys, they hear things and gossip more than females in a hair salon.

"My brother, the fag", I said to myself. I looked at Derek as his head hug down in shame. I started thinking those thoughts about Daddy again. That rotten sucka is the reason my brother sitting his gay ass up here with his head hanging down like a li'l trick. And just think! If I would'na killed him, he probably would've sent Derek up here to Tracy to be turned out. I told Derek don't stress that crap. I'll handle it, and let's just finish enjoying our day together. Besides, I had came to grips with his lifestyle sometime ago. He was still my brother and I loved him.

When we got back to Mom house we sat in my ride for a few more minutes small talking before I asked him had he told Mom what he told me. He said he hadn't, but William knew. Then I asked him how William knew. He told me before we came into William's life, he was a lonely cat who used to buy snatch and gamble real heavy on the strip. He got in debt with some hoodlums he couldn't pay, so they gave him a choice that could help clear up his debt. Now it turns out he really love Mom and want to tell her the truth, but I told him not to, not until I talk to you, because I know you would know what to do.

I told Derek to go into the house and tell William to come out to my ride. William came out with that ol' puppy dog look on his face with his head held down. I told him to get in and to pick his damn head up and look at me like a man. I asked him did he know Tracy. He answered no, but said he knew *of* her.

I asked who were the dudes that pressed up on him to box us up? He told me one of the cats was the guy who gave Derek that bad junk that almost took his mind, and the other cat was a bottom feeder pusher that used to hustle drugs and numbers around the hood near the detail shop.

William started apologizing to me over and over again. I'm sitting there looking him dead in his face with no expression on mine (like usual) thinking to myself, "I understand". I've been around saps like William before who got caught up in what we call the 'snatch trap', and they always re-act the same. Those sorry, weak suckas would suck a Johnson to avoid getting pain afflicted on that ass when the body boys (Enforcers) come.

Lastly, I asked him did he love my Mom. William looked at me and bust out crying, "So pathetic", I was thinking. But, hey, the dude was a sap. I guess it was cool, he loved her. I told William to get the hell out my ride and don't say crap to Mom about nothing.

I was convinced now. Tracy had been orchestrating all this stuff from the jump. I recall my mind racing, repeating over again, "Never underestimate an adversary", especially one like Tracy. Always play them like they're ten moves ahead of you. If I didn't have a reason to hate or despise her before, kinfolk, I had one now! That freak had to go, and I did mean sooner, not later.

No doubt Tracy was up on Derek telling me by then. That punk boy probably ran straight to her and confessed his soul, so I drove right to Tracy condo in Southfield. I needed to look into her face for any sign of her knowing what I just found out, but before I got out my ride something stopped me. "Remember, R.J.," I told myself, "Tracy is ice cold and heartless, especially when under pressure. She would read you like an open book because you would be the one out of character, searching for something in her."

I started the engine back up and drove to my condo to think the whole thing out. I realized I was no match for Tracy running up there half cocked.

Chapter 8

The Fog Lifts

To begin with, I need to understand that I cannot immediately change my present situation, but I should understand that the reason why I am experiencing this is only due to my own actions in the past. My mind is filled with delusions or positive thoughts, and the right circumstances for the karma to ripen.

On that long drive back to my place in Birmingham everything started making sense. The reason why Tracy got me a condo way the hell out there in that racistville Birmingham was to keep me out from around other blacks, especially the ones in Detroit. No matter how big of a city is, as long as niggas and fags live there it's small, because you know how both like to run their mouths. Between the pimps, dope boys, tricks, and 'hoes I would've found out way before now, but out there in Birmingham, cats ain't want no parts with coming out there for nothing. Hell, they kept their cheeks clinched tight when just driving through trying to get to Pontiac without getting harassed.

Since I was a loner she didn't have to stress about me meeting people. I guess meeting Connie really had her worried, but then I got to thinking maybe Connie was a planted stool pigeon for her. Any other chick probably would've had more of a reaction when a cat cut them loose than she had when I drove away. I done seen 'hoes damn near commit suicide when their pimp even threatened to cut them loose, but Connie just stood there like a statue when I drove off. Now, in my mind I really couldn't trust nobody. Everyone and everything around me had been strategically placed there by Tracy. She had the *control* because she had the *information*. You see, knowledge is *power*, but information is *control*. You can be smart, but if you don't have the right information, then you're screwed. The one thing I did have was that Tracy still needed was this sweet Johnson. Without it, she would lose a lot of money during the upcoming Republican convention. Hopefully it would be buy me the time I needed.

In less than three weeks we were scheduled to attend the Republican Convention in Missouri at some joint called Kemper Arena. I was determined not to get on that flight, and something was definitely going to be done about Tracy before such time. She had to go or I had to go... one of us. But I was not getting on that plane to go do anymore hunching for her.

I needed to think. Lying in bed fully clothed with the lights off listening to 105.9 WJZZ always seemed to relax me and sort of clear my mind. I had this thing I'd always done when things got tight. Instead of going off half cocked reacting like a cockroach when the lights get turned on, I always chilled—you know, did nothing but relax my mind.

I was thinking about how everything was going to end. When I was locked up, Sam and I use to somewhat talk. Well, he talked. I mainly listened. Sam use to tell me *whenever you need to come up with a plan, always think about the ending first, and work your way back to the beginning.*

I visualized Tracy being tied up to a chair with a bag over her head, me coming in and ripping the bag off, looking into that heffas cold eyes, staring into her soul before I had Sam strangle her. No words needed to be said because our eyes would've done all the talking. Her eyes would be saying, "You killed my brother and took money out my pocket!", and mine would be saying, "Say hello to your rotten brother for me, heffa!"

But before the ending could materialize I had to put a plan into place, because I had a feeling I didn't have much time. I called the only person I felt I could trust... Sam. I told him I needed him there in Michigan yesterday, and to get on a Greyhound bus booked for Toledo, Ohio, soon as we got off the phone. I told him I didn't want him coming to

56

Detroit because it was too risky, and I prefer to pick him up at the bus station in Toledo. I stressed to him not to tell anyone there in Minnesota where he was going, because I didn't need word getting back to Detroit. First part of my plan was in motion, Sam was on his way, I thought.

That next night, I guess it was a Friday around nine-thirty p.m., I was just lying on my bed with the lights off, chilling. Sam was set to arrive in Toledo that Saturday morning, so a little R&R is what I needed before the crap hit the fan. I'm chilling out like regular when I hear the front door open. I quietly grabbed my Saturday night special from under the pillow and crept slowly into the hallway up to the kitchen only to find Tracy standing there with her back to me, about to sit her pocket book and keys on the kitchen counter. Her new driver had come in also, and was standing in front of the door like a statue. That scene of him standing in my joint messed me up at first, because she never brought anybody into my pad. So something definitely was up, but, forget it. I said to myself, "If something's going down, then let's get it over with", as I firmed up my gun grip around my piece. I didn't want to use it, but I had no problem busting a cap in her after I blow up her boy standing in front my door like he bad and I was supposed to be scared. Fear wasn't in my heart anymore, and I wasn't about to put my gun down. *Her and that nigga invited themselves into my joint* was my mind set.

Tracy motioned for me to sit down. I sat on the couch in a position where I could keep my eye on the driver standing by the door as well as keep her in my vision. Tracy sat on the love seat adjacent to me and crossed her sexy legs with her head held down. Her hands placed properly on top of her thighs like Queen Elizabeth or some crap. She looked up at me and asked, "Li'l Daddy, are you okay, baby?" For a quick second I took my eyes off the driver to look directly at her then back to him. Without verbally responding, I just nodded my head letting her know I was cool. All the time I'm thinking this trick is framing me up just like I was about to do her yesterday.

Tracy was reading my body language for signs of betrayal. She wanted to hear it in my voice, but she was forgetting I was just as cool as she was, because I didn't care, either. Whenever she told me anything, from the get go I never verbally responded because talking aint' my thang. I just did what was asked of me. So, for me to start talking then would've tipped her.

Slowly and calculative she proceeded to tell me that we would be leaving for Kansas City in a week, and that she didn't want me going out anywhere until after our return. She also said she shouldn't have to explain to me how important *businesswise* that trip was for both of us. Then she got up, went to kitchen, picked her pocket book and keys up and walked toward the front door. Her driver opened the door for her, but before she stepped out she turned back to me and said, "Li'l Daddy, there's no need for you to go to Toledo in the morning... Sam won't be coming in as you so requested. Get some rest, baby." then she walked out.

Before her driver shut the door behind them he gave me a touting smile as to say, "Nigga, you just don't know who you messing with." I guess I didn't.

When that front door closed it was like someone let all the air out my body. I'm telling you, I totally deflated. This crap was getting crazy fast. How did she find out about Sam? Who the hell is this new cat, and why did he make that *off beat* comment to me? He don't have a damn thing to do with our business! I needed to find out what happen to Sam, but there wasn't anyone I could call back in Minnesota. I didn't know if he was dead, hurt, or turned on me telling one of Tracy contacts back there about me contacting him. One thing I was glad about—I didn't talk too much telling him why I needed him in Detroit.

I don't know who I'm messing with kept ringing in my head. Why did he emphasize it so venimantly? But on the other hand, that was the problem all along with me putting a plan in place. I didn't fully understand who I was dealing with—never taking into account the facts, which was I was living in a condo someone else own, the car I drove was someone else's, Mom was living in a home owned by someone else, and that someone had been manipulating my life. When they were finished with me I'm sure my family along with myself would be killed.

I had to start looking at the facts, and that was *Tracy wanted me dead.* Her only reason for not doing it sooner was she needed for me to pay back the money I had took from her when I killed her brother. After that upcoming Republican Convention my value to her would be no more.

Her new driver... who the hell is he? Where did he come from all of a sudden? It was like this dude popped up out of nowhere and Tracy is giving him the run of the plantation. I figured I had to find out who this dude was before I could do anything about getting close to Tracy. For that next two days I cased Tracy condo out. I was sure she had someone watching my spot and following me. That's the only way she would've known where I been and who I was talking to. So I decided to put on my Maxwell Smart (Get Smart) shoes and do a little investigating of my own. Instead of driving the car she bought for me, I took a cab to Southfield where I had William stash an old beat up clunker for me in Northland Mall parking lot. It was a real piece of crap car, but the engine was good and nobody paid much attention to it. I watched Tracy one night, and what I thought was the driver coming out from the under the garage of the building several times. But what tripped me out each time was, dude wasn't driving. Dude was in the back seat with Tracy, and the fag that I saw talking to Derek was driving. Ain't this a trick! All that trick Tracy was doing was setting me up like a hog being fatten up for slaughter.

The fag got to Derek telling him everything she wanted me to know. I figured then she wanted to start letting the li'l nigga who killed her brother know the truth before she kill his ass. But even more devilish than that, she wanted me to suffer knowing the truth and still be pimped out. She knew I wouldn't confront her without a way out, and she probably thought by now she had all my options covered. Now more than ever I needed to know who that new cat was Tracy had brought in the fold. Again I was face to face with a brick wall. Being a loner has a lot of disadvantages. By me not being a social creature, I didn't have anyone to turn to for any type of resource. Hell, even Sam came by way of her connections. That's why I could've kicked myself in the ass for thinking I could count on him. I needed to think, so I ditched the clunker, caught a cab, and went back to my Condo to mellow out.

The day before we were scheduled to leave for Kansas City, Tracy called me up to her Condo for one last meeting... or so I thought. I remember grabbing my Saturday night special and tucking it in between my lower back and slacks. I wasn't about to deal with this trick one on one with that busta around no more. When I got to her building, something told me not to take the gun up, so I stashed it under my driver side dashboard. When I got up to her condo, dude opened the door like Mr. Bentley or something. When I stepped in I kept my eyes locked deep into his, waiting for him to say something stupid to me, because I was in no mood to take no crap off him or Tracy.

Tracy was sitting on the couch in her usual sophisticated posture with her fake British mannerism which always bugged me out. *A black fine trick trying to act cultured*, I always thought. But, hey, that was her. She motioned for me to sit on the love seat adjacent to her, and that chump came around and sat next to her putting his arms around her at the same time. My mind was racing a hundred miles a minute, but my body demeanor and facial expression never changed. I guess they wanted to get some type of reaction out of me, but that wouldn't happen, I was too cool for that trip.

Tracy told me to take her Cadillac up to the detail shop and clean it. She told me that she wanted me to clean it, and not one of those flunkies working up there. I'm thinking to myself "This trick is either getting sloppy or trying to push my buttons. But, you know, let the games begin. She wants to play, I want to kill her. So 'f' it."

I'm sitting there looking at this cat looking back at me with a smile on his face like I'm some kind of side show freak. He threw her car keys to me like, "Here, boy. Go fetch fa yo master, nigga." I caught the keys, got up and walked out without looking back, thinking, "This trick wants to *humiliate* me now!" When I closed the door behind me, I stood there for a few seconds in silence, mad as hell, exhaling, trying to regain my unseen composure.

Standing there I could hear dude talking loudly saying he couldn't wait to hurt me. He been waiting a long time to get me back for his cousin. I'm thinking, "Who the hell is his cousin? I don't know anyone here in Detroit that I had any beef with except that drug dealer who gave my brother that bad junk that almost killed him, and that wasn't all that long ago." Seem like to me he would've came at me by now, and far as I knew Tracy and him was enemies. She wanted him dead just as much as I did, I thought.

On the way down the elevator I'm thinking, "This crap got to end now!" Before I went to get into Tracy ride, I went to mine to get my Johnny Guitar Watson eight-track. It always helped me think when I'm driving. When I got into my ride, I sat there for a few minutes, mad as hell at myself for not questioning that heffa from the jump... just going along with the flow of her program. I got so mad till I slammed both my hands down onto the steering wheel, causing the gun I had hide under the dashboard to fall out.

"THAT'S IT!" I recall yelling to myself as I picked the gun up off the floor board. The perfect plan came to me at that moment. I just needed to work more of the details out about how I would carry it out. I placed my gun back in my lower back area between my slacks and proceed to the detail shop to clean Tracy ride for our trip to the Airport tomorrow.

I hadn't been inside the detail shop since Tracy came and scooped me up. When I walked in it was like my old boss knew I was coming, along with everyone else, for that matter. It was almost like *dead man walking*, the looks they gave, but no one would say anything.

I took the Cadi to the back in my old spot where I liked to do my job. While vacuuming the back seat, the idea came to me to plant my gun between the top and bottom back seat opposite of where Tracy sat. My plan would only work if Tracy told me to ride in the back with her and her new nigga drove or sat in the front on the passenger side. It was a chance I had to bank on. I planted the gun, finished detailing her ride, then drove back round front to pay my old boss. When I tried to pay him he told me (and I quote), "Your new boss doesn't have to pay for what she own, nigga." I looked up at him and asked what he said. The oil head started stuttering "Oh, nothing. I was just rambling... you know me!"

I told him, "No, nigga, I don't know you!", and asked him again what he said, even though I heard him perfectly clear the first time. I just wanted him to confirm it, but he was too scared to.

I got back into the Cadi and proceed to make my way back to Southfield. This whole situation was starting to get crazier and crazier. Tracy owned the detail shop like everything else. That's why all them cats parted like the Red Sea that first time I saw her up there. It was clear to me that heffa was running things far beyond my comprehension. But who she was and how big was something I couldn't afford to get my mind caught up in. All I knew was that this heffa wasn't good for the future health of me or my family.

I dropped the Cadi off at Tracy's condo, walked to the lobby, and gave her keys to the doorman to take up to her. Instead of going straight home I needed to see my family. I had a feeling I may not have another chance to see them again so, I drove straight to Mom's. When I got there Mom, William, and Derek was at the dining room table playing monopoly. I couldn't believe my eyes. "My, how time brings a change", I said to myself. I use to come home and see honkies coming out her bedroom after screwing. Now she's at the dining room table with Derek and William like a family playing monopoly.

When Derek saw me he jumped up and ran to hug me. Fag or no fag, I loved my brother and he loved me, and he had always depended on me to do the right thing by taking care of him. So if I had to give my life for my family, then that's what I was prepared to do. If Mom could change the course of her life, then I could… But not until I removed the clear and present threat to my family. Strangely, it was a few things I was thankful of Tracy for—like putting us in this position to capture some type of family unit, even though she was just preparing to take it all away.

I called William to come out on the front porch. I had something I wanted to speak with him about. I told William no matter what happens to me, I need for him to take care of Derek and Mom. William looked me dead in my eyes for the first time and told me he understood whatever I had to do, and he would protect them with his life. I told him don't say that crap if he didn't mean it, because I would hold him to it, even from my grave.

He then did something that still mess with my head to this day. William gave me a hug. I would imagine it was like a father giving his son a hug before he left out to go to war for Uncle Sam or some crap. I never knew my dad, and

I surely never had a father figure, so that type of affection messed my head up. I just stood there with a confused look on my face. William was a good dude, but that hugging crap was just too much for me. All that mushy junk was for suckas.

We went back into the house. I sat around the table with them a while, watching them play their game, enjoying me a soda pop and wishing things could've been like that when I was a kid.

Chapter 9

The Plot Thickens

> *One man can conquer a thousand times a thousand men in battle, but one who conquers himself is the greatest of conquerors."*
> **The Dhammapada**

Time came for me to leave. I hugged Mom and Derek, but shook Williams' hand. "No more of that hugging crap!" I told him (with a smile on my face). Before I went home, it was just one more thing I had to do. I had to find out more about Tracy, and the one person I saw that knows a whole lot of news about her was my old boss. I drove home out to Birmingham like normal. I was sure Tracy had someone tailing me everywhere I went, so I drove home to park the ride and pretend like I was going in for the night. When I got to my building I went in like usual, went up the elevator to my floor and straight to my Condo unit. When I got inside I called a cab and told them to meet me at one of the diners off Woodward Avenue. I left back out the Condo, went down the back stairway and out the building to the spot where I told the cab company I would be.

I had the driver take me to Northland Mall to get the clunker I had stashed there, then I drove to a bar off Southfield Freeway and Six Mile Road, where I knew my old boss liked to get his drink on. When I pulled into the parking lot I spotted him sitting in his car, taking a half pint of Poko Vodka to the head. "Oil head!" I said to myself. This dude must have plenty of problems, to drink as much as he did. I got out my clunker, went up and tapped on the driver side window. That oil head jumped so high you would have thought he sobered up. First thing out his mouth was, "I can't talk to you. Leave me alone, nigga. Talking to you go get me killed." I'm standing outside his ride just looking at him. I must have stood there for twenty minutes just looking at him before he said "F-it" and told me to get in.

I told him I only had one question for him, and if he didn't want to answer, it's was cool—I understood. But me not getting any answers to my question could mean life or death to me and my family. I knew he didn't give a crap about me or my family, but I tried anyway, pulling that Orphan Annie jive on that lush... and it worked.

He took another swig on his bottle and said "'F.' it, I'm tired, anyway, of that heffa." He started to ramble all types of stuff about him working hard and that heffa taking all the money, living like a queen in Southfield with them Jews. He told me that Tracy did own the detail shop. He went on to tell me that she was the reason I got hired there against his wishes, because he wanted to hire his nephew instead of me. Tracy was involved in more than just prostitution. She was also involved with the distribution of heroin throughout parts of Chicago, Indiana, Minnesota, and Michigan. I said to myself, "I guess I don't know who I've been messing with, cause she was bigger than anything I could even imagine. But the bottom line to me was as long as that heffa was walking God's green earth, she was a threat to me and my family.

While I'm thinking all this stuff, dude was still rambling off like he had diarrhea of the mouth, until he said something that snapped me out my trance. I told the nigga to hold up and go back to what he just said. He asked "What?" I told him something about that cat from Minnesota. He said, "Oh yeah. That dude come to my town like he running stuff and that trick up there co-signing everything that nigga running down."

I told him screw the b.s.... tell me who the hell is he. He told me Tracy cop the nigga from Minnesota, Okay, I knew that. He was brought over to handle some personal business for her, and at the same time repay a debt for somebody. I asked him how the hell he knew all that. He told me dude was up at the detail shop one day with a couple of other cats. They all were up there talking junk about when they were in the joint. Dude was bragging about how much time he spent locked up since he was a juvenile, how bad he was, and now he was in town to repay some debt for a cousin.

"GOT DAMN!" I yelled, as I slammed my fist into his glove compartment door. That's probably the cousin of one of them cats I took out back in juvie. But what did he have to do with Tracy? I understood why he wanted to take me out now, and that wasn't a problem far as me comprehending. I just had a hard time connecting him with Tracy. How could a Black woman have that much juice to reach into multiple states tripped me out. Taking her and that nigga out probably wouldn't end this crap. It could actually start a wave of hungry revengeful niggas coming at me.

I had no choice. I had to take her and that nigga out. I was convinced after talking to Stan both those clowns had to go, and I would deal with whatever, whoever came at me or my family. But living in fear, or as a Johnson slinger for Tracy was something I could not live with. Then Stan said something through all his drunken rambling that gave me some sort of mental comfort. He said, "If that Heffa fell off the face of the earth yesterday, nobody would shed not one tear. No way in this world should a cunt have as much power as her and live in a man's world." Then he did a toast with his bottle in the air saying, "Here's to the death of the Queen!", taking another big swig of his Knotty Head (liquor).

I dropped my hoopty (junk car) back off at Northland Mall, then copped me a cab back to Birmingham. Sitting in back of the cab, I'm going over the plan in triples, making sure I get it right the first time, because there wouldn't be a second. The conditions for my plans had to be right. Tracy had to sit on her normal side in the backseat, dude had to sit in the front, either driving or on the passenger side, and last, if the fag came along as the driver, I would have to take him out too, right after the engine is started. Even if the fag didn't drive us to the airport, I would take him out soon as Tracy and dude was canceled.

The thinking of my plan continued. Soon as we get into her car, while still under the confines of the parking garage, I would quietly ease the gun out from between my side, shoot dude in the back of his head first, then the fag, and last, Tracy. I wanted to look into that tricks eyes one last time.

I pictured every motion of the event in my mind. Slide gun out, pop dude first, the sound of the gun would freeze Tracy and the fag in the front seat for three seconds, just enough time to bang, bang, boogie. I wouldn't have to worry about the sound bringing attention, the parking garage was below ground with solid cement all around, perfect spot for an ambush.

I snuck back into my building, up the back stairs, and straight to my unit. When I went to slide my key in the door lock, the door pushed open, freezing me in my step. I stood there for a few seconds, debating whether to enter or not. Then I said, "Screw it!" When I pushed that door open I almost crap on myself when I heard that familiar deep voice hit me.

"What's up li'l nigga?"

"SAM!" I yelled! It was Sam, sitting on my couch, eating a big healthy sandwich, drinking my root beer soda pop. I asked him what was he doing there, what happened to Toledo? Sam told me about fifteen minutes after we hung up he gets this call from a woman he do muscle work for occasionally to make a run over to Chi Town on her behalf. He said he told her he couldn't because he had to handle some business in Toledo on that Saturday for a friend, and could her business possibly wait until he got back? The woman made him a sizable offer to clear his calendar for the next couple of days to go to Chi Town to handle her business. He said he couldn't refuse that much loot, plus all expenses paid to chill afterwards in the Chi, too. I understood with Sam money talked and personal crap didn't pay a damn thing. He told me the folks who hired him still thought he was in Chi, but he managed to slip out to drive over to Michigan in a car he kept stashed in a garage for emergency purposes, just in case some heavy crap went down.

I asked Sam did he remember the dude cousin from back in juvie that I canceled. Sam said he knew *of* him. He said dude ran things on his side of juvie hall, and had approached him before he got out for permission to cancel me, but he wouldn't give the nod. When dude got out juvie, he sent word throughout the Twin I was no longer untouchable, but by then I had already moved to Detroit.

While Sam was saying all, that I'm thinking to myself, "How did dude get hooked up with Tracy?" Then Sam snapped! "YOU KNOW WHAT?", he said to me. "That female who I do work for back in the Twin knows that nigga. She uses niggas like that to Boguard (Bogart) block boys (run corner drug dealers of their block) in other cities before her people set up shop."

Then it all came together. Tracy knew just who to get to take me out when she was finished with me. She had been getting jail house updates on me on the regular when I was on lock down. The crazy thing about dude was, I knew back in juvie that cat was go be a problem, and should've dealt with him back then. Now the chicken had come home to roost.

Since the crap in juvie died down so smoothly I let my guard down thinking it was a wrap (finished). Now I'm again thinking if I take Tracy out tomorrow evening will it truly be over? I ran down on Sam everything from day one,

69

including about killing Daddy, and Tracy being his sister. We figured whoever Tracy had tailing me saw me on the payphone talking to someone, and told her. She took a chance it was him, and had her connect in the Twin call him to pick his brain first, then make him an out of town offer to get him out the way.

I told him how connected she was throughout parts of the Mid East, then I asked would it be a smart move to make a move on her. Sam paused for a minute. He told me it's never a smart move to move on someone like her without permission, but if it's his life versus someone else's, and those was the only two choices given, long as it's understood it's a price to pay for every action. I had to be willing to pay for the action I was planning to make. Then he said, "Besides, no Alpha male Negros like taking orders from a bitch, anyway", laughing afterwards.

Sam also told me (in a joking way) don't be surprised if it's him they pay to come after me, and for some reason I felt he wasn't really joking. But I guess that's understandably part of the chance I had to take for my action.

I laid down my plan to Sam in detail. Everything was cool until he asked me what was I planning on doing with the bodies afterwards? I looked at him like I was crazy. Crap, I didn't think about that. He said after I cancel them I can't just leave the bodies in the car like no one's going to question or investigate the crap. I had to get rid the bodies. Plus, if the door man (which was the elevator attendant also) seen me with them, he could be a witness for the cops if they found two or three bodies in the car, and mine not being one of them. Also, even though the garage is concrete enclosed, the sound of the blast still can carry.

Sam then reached down into a green duffle bag, unzipped it and pulled out a midnight black gun with what looked to me like a tip on the end. He said it was a new toy he picked up on while honing his skills at the gun range. It was a silencer. Sam said niggas wasn't up on that new tip, taking marks out like a Ninja with a gun. I had seen guns like that on TV, and heard about cats using potatoes, but what Sam had was the real deal on some James Bond type tip. Regular cats in the hood couldn't get their hands on a hookup like that, but then again, Sam wasn't no regular hood cat.

After giving Sam a crash course of the layout of the building, he came up with a new plan that included taking care of the bodies. We went over his plan in detail, covering all scenarios top to bottom. I gained an appreciation for how detail that big black Negro was when it came to handling his business. I also realized then why he got paid as much as he did. Sam wasn't no joke when it came to handling his business, I would soon find out.

It was getting late. Sam left to go case Tracy building out for himself (at least that's what he told me). I packed up my suits and a few other items Tracy wanted me to bring on this trip, including a red neck tie representing the Republican Party. Afterwards I took a hot bath, and then laid out on my bed, listening to WJZZ until I finally fell asleep.

I awaken the next morning to someone shaking my feet trying to wake me up. It was Tracy, sitting on the end of my bed.

"Sleep well, li'l Daddy?" she said to me. Before I answered her I got up and did my regular routine, which was going to the restroom taking me a good healthy piss. Before I stepped back into my bedroom I peeped round the corner to see if she brought that nigga along with her this time, and sure enough, he was standing in front'a the door, like some titan fresh out of gladiator school. "Cool", I said to myself as I walked back into the bedroom and sat on the end of the bed next to Tracy. She told me to be at her place at one p.m. on the dot—not a minute late. Our plane would be taking off at

71

4:10 p.m., so that allowed us plenty of time to get there and check in. All the while she's telling me what she want me to do, I'm thinking, "Where the hell is Sam, and how can I let him know what the schedule is?"

After she finished laying out her agenda to me, her and dude proceeded to exit my crib, and again, before that nigga closed my door behind them, he looked back at me with a threatning look that was clear in its message. He wanted to let me know my time was coming. In response to his attempt, I grabbed my balls and shook them at him letting him know I didn't give a care about his eye ball threats, and he could hug these nuts fa real. Now I'm thinking to myself, "This trick really believes I don't know by now who I'm messing with", and that was fine by me.

I got myself together as Tracy requested. I put all my gear in my ride, then just sat there for a few seconds, taking deep breaths and running through the cancellation process in my mind before we get down. But where was Sam? I hadn't heard from him since last night. But the show had to go on, with or without him. *Or maybe he was setting me up.* I didn't really know at that point. All I did know was Tracy couldn't let anything happen to me until I fulfilled her contracts in Kansas City. So I was guaranteed to get a shot at them with my half of a plan. The hell with getting rid of the bodies.

It seems like I drove all the way over to Tracy's place in slow motion and blindfolded. When I got there cops were all around the place, even blocking off the entrance/exit to the parking garage. "What's going on here?" I said to myself. I got out my ride and pushed to the front of the crowd, trying to get the scoop on what was going down. I saw the day time doorman standing outside the lobby door with his hands cross, head down, trying to puff on a cigarette, looking nervous as hell. I waved my hands up trying to get his attention. When he looked up to take a puff

I got his attention, motioning to him come see me. When he came over to speak with me, I asked him what was going down. He told me my girl and some dude had got killed execution style down below in the parking garage. He stated when he made his rounds checking the garage he found her and dude in her Cadi, heads damn near blown off. I asked him did anyone hear anything. He said no. He said he seen when they arrived back to the building driving down to the parking garage, but didn't see or hear anything else. He also said that Tracy's condo had been broken into and ram sacked like someone was looking for something important. The detectives said it appeared her condo had been broken into before the murder had been committed.

I'm telling you, if I didn't believe in God before, I did then. No doubt in my mind it was Sam that took both of them out like a Ninja with a gun. I laughed to myself.

I drove back to my place with a lot of questions swirling around in my head. Who did it? If Sam, *why without me*? What was they looking for in her Condo? And would they be looking for *me* next? Whatever the answers was to those questions, I didn't waste too much time stressing over them. It was what it was. I was just happy that heffa and mutha was canceled.

When I made it back to my place, the first person I called was Connie. I told her all my business had been handled, and my mind was clear now. I went to pick her up and it was like we never missed a beat. We went back to my place, ordered Chinese food, listened to some jazz, and chilled out all night lying on top of the covers with our clothes on, content.

That next morning I heard a knock at the door. I went to grab my Saturday night special and remembered; my piece was in Tracy's car. "Oh, CRAP!" I screamed, waking Connie. "What's wrong, baby?" she asked. I told her "Nothing.. I forgot something in a friend's car." Then I got up to see who was at the door.

When I opened the door no one was there... only a box on the floor in front my door. "DAMN!" I said to myself. That crap there could be a bomb or something. But I picked it up anyway, brought it in, sat it on the floor in front of me, and flopped down on the couch. By this time Connie came out the bedroom wiping her eyes, trying to focus on me sitting on the couch, looking down at that box, debating whether to open it or not. I looked up at Connie then back down to the box and said "Forget it!" I started opening it. When I moved that last flap back, Connie and I jumped, screaming, "WHAT THE HELL!" at the same time. Someone had sent my gun and thousands of dollars in cash! I knew it had to be nobody but Sam! He was the only one who knew where I hid my gun in Tracy's back seat. There was a note also, saying I should take my family, the cash, and move away from Michigan and don't look back.

I did just that. But first I asked Connie to move to Atlanta with me. At first she hesitated until I told her I heard Atlanta had some pretty good Black colleges where she can complete her schooling at, plus the weather was warm all year round, not like these nasty winters in Michigan. She agreed to move with me under the condition that whatever I had dealt with in my past was over with and wouldn't come back to haunt us. I told her the only thing I could guarantee in this dirty world is to do everything in my power to give her the best life I possibly could. The way Connie looked at me made me realize for the first time in my life what real love is, and to this day she is the only woman that I have or ever will love.

I couldn't leave Detroit without my family. I truly thought convincing them to move to Atlanta with Connie and I would've been much more challenging, but it wasn't. Not only did Mom and Derek hop on the opportunity. but William, too. William had over thirty-eight years with Ford and said he had wanted to retire for sometime, but didn't have anything else going on in his life to live for but work. Since Mom came into his life, she gave him something to live for. Living without her, he said, would be like the Lord taking his breath away.

You know me, when he was saying all that sappy crap, I was thinking to myself "Boy, is this sucka snatch whipped!" As for my brother Derek, he was happier than a sissy-in-a-bag-of-pickles to move. So I packed up my woman and family and moved them to Atlanta, GA.

Chapter 10

A New Beginning

There may be things present in our lives and our habits that we are not happy about. We want change, yet as hard as we try, sometimes, we are just not seeing the level of profound change we desire.

When we got to Atlanta, I bought Mom and William a home in a nice quiet suburb outside the city, about what seem like a two hour drive in Atlanta traffic from the place I purchased for Connie and myself in a nice quiet, exclusive, all white community. I was already accustomed to living in exclusive white areas, so fitting in wasn't a problem for me, but a big adjustment for Connie. Back in Detroit she lived on the Westside with her grandmom off Outer Drive and McNichols. It wasn't a really bad area, but it wasn't nothing like our crib in Atlanta.

I remember Connie telling me that her Grandmom would always call her her little 'Ms. Princess', and said that a Black knight in shining armor would take her away and grant her the wishes of her heart. Who would've ever thought a Black Carolina nigga, son of a whore like me, would be a Black knight. But I guess you don't have to be Saint Benedict to be a blessing for someone.

William and Mom settled in quite well. For a cat who cleaned floors and toilets for over thirty-five years at Ford, William had managed to save up a nice nest egg, on top of his retirement check which came ever month on time like clockwork. They opened up an office building cleaning service, and within a year's time had taken on six employees to manage the eight full time buildings they maintained monthly. *"Mom turned out to be a better business woman than whore"*, I would joke to myself. She had negotiated a deal with the building managers to contract out their cleaning services to her instead of taking on the overhead and liability responsibilities for the buildings general cleaning. I recall her telling me when she told them White folks they didn't have to worry about employees wages, benefits or retirement, they was ready to sign her contract in crayon. And, mind you, this was way before *out-sourcing* was even thought of.

Derek loved Atlanta. He enrolled at Morehouse College, along with Connie. Derek fitted in to his new environment too good. It turned out that Atlanta was becoming a hot spot for young educated urban gays. Although back then it wasn't as open as it is now, still Atlanta for Derek truly turned out to be like being in a barrel of hot dill pickles.

Connie switched her curriculum from business to chemistry major. I didn't have any idea what the hell chemistry was or what type of job it would get someone, but as long as my woman was happy pursuing whatever it was, it was cool with me. She would come home from school with all these thick books with all types of formulas and crap in them. I had set up one of our bedrooms as a study for her to do her home work in. My baby would be in there for hours studying her ass off. She was just as committed to her education as she was to me, and I didn't mind that one bit. Besides, I enjoyed my quiet time alone with my jazz and thoughts. Plus, Connie always gave me plenty of room to breathe. I think that's why she has been the only woman I've ever loved to this day. From the moment she came up to me in White Castle, somehow it just felt right, even though I fought like hell against even talking to her. Connie could read me like an open book. The cool thing about that has always been she never pressured me to talk about nothing. She just gave me the space I needed to work things out myself. Beside the change in Mom, Derek and Connie made my life complete, and everything in my past less memorable and painful than they actually had been.

As for me, with some of the money I had left over, I opened up my own auto detailing shop. Since that was one of the only things that had always seemed to relax me, it was only fitting, and Atlanta was perfect, due to the weather being as cool as it was all year round in comparison to Michigan. I heard William say one time, "Do what you love and you'll live a long time." And let me emphasize that was just one of a few things I ever took from a snatch-whipped sap like him. (Laughing).

My detail shop was set up out of an old shipping warehouse. All my customers were either from the area's Ford, GM, small car lots, or business folks. I was able to sustain my business without walk-ins. I had enough business from legit folks till I didn't need no dope boys or pimps hanging round my spot, which was just the way I wanted it. The last thing I wanted for my business was to be like the detail shop back in Michigan, with hustlas hanging around like wet clothes on a clothes line. My shop wasn't upscale, but it damn sho wasn't ghetto, kinfolk!

I had three li'l cats working for me—Glen, Charles, and Tim. Glen was the hot headed one who was always fighting with other hood cats about dumb stuff before I gave him a job.

The first time I saw that dude I had taken a wrong turn ending up in this messed up neighborhood. I was looking for this Independent Allstate Insurance Company agent whom had a schedule pickup detailing appointment. I spotted Glen surrounded by these jokers about to get whipped, or so I thought. These three cats had him hemmed up on a corner with his back against the stop sign pole. When I saw them I knew right away what was about to go down, so I pulled my ride over to see how the fight was going to play out. I had no plans of interfering, because a cat got to get himself out of mess on his own, because seven times out of ten he done did something crazy to be in a position like that.

Now Glen was no big kid, he was only about 4'9" & a buck fifty, but he put a whipping on them cats that had me laughing my tail off. That li'l joker turned into a wild boar pig when they cornered him. When I figured the cats who tried to hem him up had enough, I got out my ride and yelled, "HEY, WHAT THE HELL YA'LL DOING". Those li'l rascals jumped up off the ground and broke camp like li'l gals with their soft peepees tucked between their thighs. Actually, they should've been thanking me for saving them from anymore of that ol' fashion ass whipping Glen was putting on their asses.

I walked up to Glen, asked him if he knew where the Allstate spot was I was looking for. He told me how to get there. I gave him my phone number and fifty dollars. I told him when he was ready to get off those streets give me a call... I had a job for him. The next day he called, and it's been all good with that joker ever since. He became the straight li'l brother I never had. I even helped him and his gal get into a really nice apartment, and he's been loyal to me even to this day. Connie and I became god-parents to their two beautiful daughters.

Charlie was a big young cat who was black like midnight. He reminded me of Sam. He was quiet in a shy way, and you never knew what he was thinking. I like that young boy because of those similarities. Don't trip now. I met Charlie while Connie and I were having lunch at Roscoe Chicken and Waffles between her classes. Connie was the one who actually pointed him out to me. This big young cat was in a white shirt, dusty black pants (looking like he had been rolling around in flour) and a black plastic apron wrapped around his waist, bussing tables. When he got to our table, Connie asked him his name. Dude was surprisingly quite polite to her. He told her his name, and then said "Yes ma-am/no-ma-am" behind every question. I'm thinking to myself, "This is the biggest, most respectful young cat I've ever seen in my life." Connie looked at me smiling, and immediately I knew what she was thinking. I wrote my number on a napkin and slid it to him. Then Connie told him when he was ready to do something different in the line of employment to call that number, we had a job waiting on him. Now I'm thinking, "What is this '*we*' stuff? She got a mouse or French taxi cab driver in her pocket book or something?" I didn't verbally say a thing. I just kept eating my lunch.

The next day he called, so I picked him up at the Waffle house and he, too, has been with me to this day. Later I found out Charlie had done some time in juvie for breaking bones on a couple of kids when he was in sixth grade, but that didn't bother me. I wasn't exactly Beaver Clever my damn self. Plus, I liked him because he gave my woman lots of respect. In fact, Charlie became over protective of Connie. When we would take our employees and their gals out for different events, nobody bet'n not say nothing to her disrespectful, or that big ol' dude would stand up on they ass—ya hear me, kinfolk? Connie eventually introduced him to a beautiful Mocha sister who attended college with her. The chick was a few years older than Charlie, but it still worked. They had one child, a beautiful little girl, and yes, we became god-parents to her also.

Last but not least, Tim! Tim was a character that was always in some crap. This li'l cat always had a scam or hustle going on. I was walking with a couple of business clients (who were actually showing me the spots for the first time). Downtown, through Atlanta's Underground, is where I met that li'l hustling behind cat. Dude had got hemmed up by the cops for trying to pick-pocket an undercover police woman. They had his li'l ass handcuffed, and his face was smashed up against the concrete wall with his legs spread. I told the cats I was with to hold up while I strolled over to one of the officers. I asked one of the officers could if I speak with him for a quick second. He acknowledged me, and we stepped to the side. Without saying anything else to him, I wrote my phone number down on back of one of the dudes I was with business card, gave it to him and asked him to turn Tim over to me. I told him I would give him a job, and if he ever see him down there again, he can call that number and I will come to the police station and turn *myself* in. The officer looked at me like I was out my mind Then he looked back over at Tim, then back to me standing there with no expression… my face cold as ice. He flipped my business card over, then flipped back to the number on back. He asked me was it my business on front the card? I said "No Sir". Then he said, "Forget it. I got no time to be messing around with li'l pick pocketing punks like him anyway." But if he ever saw Tim down there again, I would be getting a call to come down to the station.

I thanked him, grabbed Tim by the back of his tee shirt, and took him along with us. My prospected business clients were a little uncomfortable, but I didn't care. Giving a kid like Tim a chance was more important to me at the time than networking to get their detailing business. I felt I had to help that li'l cat, and to this day that insane li'l dude has been with us, but he's still always in some crap (although he did keep it away from the shop). I guess some folks can't change and it's not my job to try changing them, but to show them something different to choose from. Besides, without him up at the shop it probably would be boring, cause that li'l cat always into something harmless and stupid. Thank God that fool didn't have any kids… (smiling!)

Chapter 11

The More Things Change...

> *It may appear that Karma is happening to us, as if some outside force is causing good things or bad things to come to us. However, it is really our own inner conditionings and processes that are leading us to experience outer effects or consequences in relation to our own actions.*

After being in Atlanta for over a year I thought the drama in my life was over. I had managed to get my family out of that hell hole of a city (Detroit), purchased my Moms a home, put my brother and woman through college, and start my own successful business. But something still wasn't right. One of the things that still haunted me was I left too many loose ends and questions unanswered, and no sooner than those thoughts entered my mind it happened.

I went to visit Mom and to check on Derek. Even though Connie and Derek attended Morehouse at the same time, we didn't see much of him (with him being a real college gay socialite, ya know). When I got to Mom's place, the first thing she said soon as I stepped in the house was, "Thank God you're here, R.J. Your brother has been upstairs crying all day like he lost his best friend or something."

When I got up to Derek's room, I found him sitting on the floor in a pair of white cotton draws and a wife beater tee shirt, staring at a picture frame he held in his left hand. I asked him what was wrong with him. He didn't answer except for saying, "Nothing!" I walked over and snatched the picture frame out his hand.

"What tha...?", I yelled! It was a photo of Derek and that fag back in Detroit, all hugged up and stuff like two tricks. Before I knew it, I backhand slapped my li'l brother so hard he flew up and back across his bed! Then I jumped across the bed and snatched his ass up by his wife beater, screaming at his li'l sissy behind. "**I know you not crying about that fag! FORGET THAT SISSY ASS HOMO!**"

Like the li'l girl my brother was, he yelled back at me, **"I loved him, R.J.!"**

I let go of his shirt. causing him to fall back onto the floor while still screaming at his ass, **"You *loved* him! What the hell you talking about, Derek? You *loved* him?"**

Derek looked up at me with tears running down his face, screaming back at me, "He's dead, R.J., he's *dead*! somebody *killed* him!"

I fell back onto the bed. I asked Derek what the hell was he talking about. He said he got a phone call from some friends he knew back in Michigan telling him his boy had been found ass bone naked with a bullet through the back of his skull. "What the hell!" I said to myself. This mess ain't over! One of the loose ends I didn't deal with was that sissy boy. He knew too much and now I find out Derek was still creeping with that snitch ass sissy boy, which meant he knew where we ran to. Whoever popped his ass probably questioned him first by the way they executed him, so I figured I would be getting a Hallmark card soon or a fish in the mail box. I started thinking about what Sam jokingly said. He would probably be the one to carry out the hit on me if paid enough. I wasn't worried about me... I was more concerned about my promise to Connie about this mess being over. I brought her a long way on that promise all because I jumped the gun, leaving without putting the time in to think about things. I should have dealt with that sissy right after finding out about Tracy and dude getting canceled, but I didn't.

Another thing that bothered me that I just brushed aside was the whereabouts of Tracy's little blue and black books. There was a lot of information in there that could get a lot of important folks in high places messed up. Someone had those books—I was convinced of that fact. Just *who* was the question.

I picked Derek up off the floor, apologized, then hugged him. I told him it wasn't a smart thing, keeping in contact with dude, but, then again, I never told him his friend's involvement with Tracy. I just figured dude would get the hint after her untimely demise and stay away from Derek in fear of what could happen to him. I swallowed my tongue, apologized to Derek for the loss of his friend. I wasn't apologizing to him because I meant it. I did it out of respect for my little brother. (I laughed jokily saying to myself, "This li'l ferry can be the biggest freak, and be with all the men in the world he wants to, but he's still my li'l brother, and I still would give my life for his li'l ferry ass.")

I went back down stairs to say bye to Mom. While she was rambling off at the mouth about some harmless dumb crap William had done, my mind was occupied, peeking out the curtains for anything out of the ordinary. Then Mom said something that snapped me back. "BOY, You're acting just like that nosy hag, Mrs. Clair, next door... in everybody business, but couldn't remember her own name when the cops came knocking on her screen door when that boy got stabbed in front of her yard a couple weeks ago."

"Mrs. Clair?", I said to myself. If anyone would've come round here that didn't belong that nosey bat would surely have the 411, so I headed next door to peep her out.

Walking up the steps to Mrs. Clair's front porch was scary! It was almost like walking up to the door of the Adams family home, anticipating Lurch answering the door. Her porch was encased with really dark black tinted screen all around it, where you couldn't see in day or night, from any angle. Mom said she thinks Mrs. Clair sleeps on that porch all night just so she could see what's going on. And to top that off, it was always dark in her house, like she didn't have any lights, or was too cheap to pay her light bill.

When I reached her front screen door I heard a voice...
"What you want, Willa Mae Jones son?"
"Is that you, Mrs. Clair?"
"I don't know, boy. What you want?"

I asked Mrs. Clair if I could come in and speak with her for a few. She told me, "No! Not unless you got some Bugle Boy tobacco in yo pocket!" I told her I didn't have no tobacco on me, but if she spoke with me for a few, I'd bring her some back next time I came see my Mom. Mrs. Clair told me to get away from her garret (front porch) and don't come back until I got her Bugle Boy tobacco. Then we can talk about that long black car that's been sitting up the street watching my Mom house the last couple evenings.

Without saying another word, I left to go get Mrs. Clair's tobacco. On that short drive to one of the neighborhood stores all I was thinking was, "Why can't I get away from my past? Why can't I live a normal, quiet life like regular folk? What I'm going to tell Connie?" All those and more unanswered questions filled my head so much until I started to get a migraine headache. I kept telling myself, "R.J., calm down. Don't jump to conclusions without having all the facts. That car could've been casing someone else's pad, not your Mom, man. That ol' hag (Mrs. Clair) could be seeing things, dude. Hell, that black screen she sitting behind, how in the world could she see anything? So, just be cool, Richard Jones, until you really know what's going down, baby."

I copped (bought) Mrs. Clair's Bugle Boy tobacco, then made my way back to her pad. As I was making my way up the steps to her porch, I heard her say, "Come on in, Willow Mae Jones boy. The screen door is unlatched, and boy, you *better* have my Bugle Boy, ya hear?"

When I got inside of Mrs. Clair porch and looked out the screen, I could see she had a very good view of the entire street. Hell, she had a better view than a NASA satellite. She was sitting there in the dark on a metal green outdoor swing looking couch, bi-focal glass barely hanging onto the edge of her nose, dirty white scarf on her head, and some old dingy socks and house shoes. Mrs. Clair looked like she was about eighty-five years old.

Mrs. Clair looked me up and down, then ordered me to give her Bugle Boy to her and sit down on the chair next to her swing.

She took her tobacco, then pulled out her tobacco pipe and begins stuffing it with tobacco. After it was packed she lit it up and took a fat hit of it like a junkie taking that first hit of crack. I was sitting there like, "DANG! Mrs. Clair getting her blaze on fa real, kinfolk!"

After Mrs. Clair got her head right, she turned her attention to me. She asked me, "What do that big black boy in that long black car want with you?" I asked her how she knew whoever it was was looking fa *me*? She told me don't act crazy with her. She said she ain't never seen that car round there before until us moved in the neighborhood. Plus that car had a out'a state license plate on it. I asked Mrs. Clair how she knew the car had out of state plates, and how did she know the person inside was a big black man? She said that big black boy was mannish (disrespectful). He had been sitting his tail up there so long till he musta had to pee, so he got his tail out and pee'd right there on the curve like he owned the dangone street or something, big black bastard!" I wanted to laugh out loud, but I kept it inside.

Mrs. Clair was out her tree house (crazy). Then she said when he was pee-peeing, she got up and went closer to the front screen trying to get a better look, because it looked like he had a long ding-a-ling, and she hadn't seen nothing like that since her last late husband Riley Charles died. "That no good black bastard!"

"Okay, Mrs. Clair", I said. Anyway, she continued, "When he got back into that long black car, he started it up and drove pass here, that's when I seen the license plate." I asked her did she recollect (remember) what state it was? She paused, picked up her pipe and took another long hit and then coughed. After her long drag (puff), she said she didn't remember, but she does know that it begin with an M.

"An M... Michigan?... Minnesota?" I asked her. She said she didn't know, but she did recollect they looked black and white. "Black and white license plates..." I said to myself, "That's Michigan! ...Can't be Sam. Why would Sam be in a car with Michigan plates on it?" I could see him driving something with Illinois, Minnesota, or Indiana... but Michigan didn't make any sense.

I gave Mrs. Clair twenty dollars for some more tobacco and thanked her for looking out for my Mom. Before I walked out her screen door she stopped me in my tracks with a warning.

"Willow Mae Jones boy! ...Have you ever thrown a rock in a calm creek of wata, boy?"

"Yes, Ma'am", I said back.

Then she continued. When ya throw a rock in a calm puddle of wata, soon as it hits the wata it disturbs the calmness of the wata, and create ripples in the wata that moves out from the centa (center) of where the rock went in at. The ripples come out, and then they return to the centa from which they came, and calmness is then restored. What you have to do, Willow Mae Jones boy, is deal with the ripples that you created before the calmness can be restored to yo life, boy! Then only can you and yo family enjoy calmness. Now get off my garret (porch), boy, and tell yo brother Derek to keep that racket (noise) down! Him and them other sissy boys be out there in that drive way on Saturday night with all that racket. I be seeing them!"

On the long drive back to my place I wrecked my brain trying to figure out who from Michigan could be looking for me. If Derek had only kept his gay ass away from Tracy's punk boy, none of this would be happening. Then I thought about what Mrs. Clair said about disturbing the calmness of the water. She was right. This wasn't his fault... this was mine. I should've dealt with that sissy myself before I skated (left) out'a Detroit. Whoever iced (killed) that sissy made him talk first   That's the only reason why they know where we escaped to.

But what do they want? I never seen any faces. The only faces I ever seen was those famous dead white boys (money), and those snobby white tricks I was laying pipe to.

I needed to think. When I arrived home Connie was in the kitchen finishing up dinner. Her eyes were deep in her chemistry book and her hands tossing up a big bowl of salad. I told her I wasn't hungry right then, and could we maybe eat later. My head was hurting, and I needed to lay down for a few. Connie took one look at me and knew I needed my space. She told me she had bought me a new Bobby Humphrey eight-track tape, and it was already cued up in the player in the bedroom. She thought maybe after dinner we could lay in bed like we use to and listen to it, but she has a lot of studying to do, so I should go chill out in the bedroom alone and vibe to it.

"Man," I thought to myself, "What did I do to deserve a woman like this? I can't let any part of my past touch any parts of her soul, even if it means giving up my life."

Back in the bedroom I took my usual position lying across the bed. Bobby Humphrey was sounding sweet in the eight-track. Her flute was luring me into that too familiar zone... the one where I escape to when I needed to engulf myself in deep thought.

I started from the end and worked my way back, like I was taught. The end for me was when I found out Tracy was dead. Ok, someone ransacked her crib before they murdered her. What was they looking for? Did they find what they was looking for? Why did they torture the fag? What did he have to do with all this? He was just a worker. And most importantly, where was Sam that night?

I must have beaten down every scenario and combination in my mind trying to figure out the answers to my questions. Ever which way I framed, they lead me to a brick wall.

Finally I got up, saying "Screw it!", sitting on the edge of the bed). I was tired of beating myself up, so I came to the conclusion that whoever, whatever, will be revealed in time, and then I'll deal with it.

I remembered a scene from watching the animal channel. A mongoose never goes in for the kill on a cobra until the cobra's mouth is open and he's in mid air trying to strike. That's what I'll do... Just like the mongoose—wait until whoever makes a move, than I'll counter. It was risky, but my only option at the time.

So I got up, went into the living room where Connie was sitting on the love seat, legs folded Indian style underneath her fine ass, sipping a glass of red wine, head stuck in her book. I walked over to her, bent down on my knees in front of her, placed my arms around her fine perfectly shape ass, gently grip both her cheeks with my hands and laid my head in her lap. She put her book down, ran her fingers through my hair, and in that soft, sweet voice of hers, told me she loved me and that I'll figure it out, whatever it was that was troubling me.

"I got to get up," I said to her. When I stretched my arms out to her, my hands went between seams of the pillows. I felt something hard like a book or something. When I pulled it out, it was Tracy blue book! "Aw, man!" I said. I reached in between the seams of the pillows again and pulled out her black book! "Aw, man!" I said again! "I'm dead!" I said to myself.

Connie looked at me and said, "R.J., I don't want to know what those are. All I know is you promised me you was done with whatever you was into, and judging by your response to finding those books, something's not over."

I didn't know what to say. I asked Connie to trust me—the less she knew the better. This was something I felt I would have to leave Atlanta to deal with.

I couldn't believe it. That freak Tracy stuck those books in my couch probably that morning before we we're to leave for Kansas. She must have known something was about to go down for her to stash them in my crib. Whoever killed her and dude must have broken into her joint (condo) first, ransacking it looking for them. But why they would kill her before getting their hands on them didn't make any sense to me.

I told Connie I needed her to go back to Detroit and stay with her grandma for about a week or until I deal with this thing once and for all. Connie didn't like it, but she didn't question me. She just went into the bedroom and shut the door. I could hear her in there crying, but the situation was what it was, and I couldn't let feelings get in the way now. This thing was about life or death. I knew sending Connie back to Detroit she would be safe. I learned over time the place to hide something precious is right under someone's nose, just like that heffa Tracy did me.

The next morning I told Connie I would be driving her to school. She told me she wasn't going to start living in fear, and I told her I wasn't going to take any chance on living without her. After that response I could've spread her on toast.

After I dropped Connie off at school I made my way to the shop. When I arrived there, Charlie told me some cat in a black Eldorado had been circling pass the shop too many times like he was looking for something. Tim then said "Yeah, dude plates said 'Minnesota'." I asked Tim was he sure the plates was Minnesota. Then he reminded me how good he was with numbers by telling me the license plates number. At that moment Glen ran in yelling, "Charlie" (before seeing me) "Oh, hey boss! Didn't know you was here. But that black Eldog (Eldorado) is parked outside in front the shop." Me and the boys quickly walked to the front of the shop where who do you think was standing there?... Sam!

Tim asked him, "Who the heck is you, man... driving pass my place of business like you the po po (police)? Sam gave Tim a look I was too familiar with, so I quickly stepped in and told all three of my boys to get back to work before Sam lit (beat up) into Tim ass. But Charlie, he just stood there looking Sam dead in his eyes, not saying a word. Sam stared back harder, until I told Charlie again to get his ass back to work like I told him. Now Charlie was a big young cat, but Sam would have ate his ass up and spit him out like dog crap. I couldn't let that happen.

After me and Sam was alone he turned and asked me, "How ya been, potnah?"

I responded, "Like I look, big nigga!" He smiled, and then told me I look like I been doing well for myself up until then. Sam continued by telling me it wasn't a good idea for my li'l brother Derek to keep in contact with that fag. I agreed with him. He said someone has Tracy's blue and black book, and the people who hired him need those books right away. His instructions were *if the books can't be found, kill everyone who ever worked for Tracy.* Sam then said he did something he has never done for anyone. He told me he vouched for me that I didn't have Tracy books, but if I had any knowledge of where they could be, I would tell him.

Sam was letting me know that he put his ass on the line for me. If I don't help him find those books I would be on Tracy ex-workers kill list, and he would also be marked for death for standing up for me.

I could've easily given Sam the books, but something told me not too. Sam was a hired gun, and whoever commissioned him probably has already ordered all Tracy workers killed anyway after the books are found. I figured by holding onto the books, it would give me enough time to think about my next move ,which could be my *only*. I told Sam I appreciated him putting his ass on the line for me, and I certainly didn't want to sound ungrateful, but I didn't ask him to vouch for me. Sam told me he understood, but he also knew me, how I kept to myself, and wouldn't have got involved in the details on how Tracy ran her business.

I asked Sam to give me a couple of days to see what I could come up with. I told him I would go back to Detroit to see what I could dig up, starting at the detail shop. He told me he had a couple of appointments (hits) to keep back in Chicago and then Detroit. So we agreed to meet back up at my shop in Atlanta in a couple of weeks.

When Sam left it felt like all the air left out my body. I fell back in my chair behind my desk, closed my eyes for what seemed like forever, until my phone rang. "DAMN" I said softly to myself. "Hello." It was my Mom. She was hysterical. I asked her to calm down and tell me what was wrong! Mom told me Derek was packing his bags talking about going back to Detroit. I told mom to put his ass on the phone right then and now. Derek got on the phone, crying his ass off like a li'l girl. I asked him what was wrong with him, bugging out about going back to that hell hole of a city, Detroit. Derek said he wanted to go to his (punk boy) friend funeral. I told him I didn't think it was a good idea at the time, and he could possibly wait until after the funeral. Then he could just pay his respect to the grave site. Derek was tripping. He said he wanted to go to the funeral, and he didn't need my permission, or Mom's. I told him to just hold up until I get there before he go off half cocked, and I'll give him some money and help him make plans. After I hung up with him, it came to me... I needed a good reason to go back to that jive city, and maybe this was it. If I had just showed up there with no reason and started asking questions it would look suspicious. So maybe this could be a good way to kill two birds with one stone. Derek could do his gay thang and I could snoop around on the visit tip.

After I hung up with Derek I again fell back into my chair. "DAMN!" It seemed like one thing after the other was going down in six seconds after the other. I needed time out of mind to pull everything together... a good plan of attack on how I was going to pull this crap off. I had the books, but I needed someone to plant them on—a "fall guy". But there was no one I could think of that I hated that much, to let them take the rap for what I had done with their life, so this one I would have to make up as I go.

Before I left the shop I called in my boys. I told them to just listen and don't interrupt me or ask me any questions during or after I say what have to say. I told Charlie he was in charge. If anything happen to me all three had to promise me they would take care of Connie. I told them that the shop would be theirs, and they had to continue running it professionally and together. I made it clear to them that the shop was something they could build on, so they or their kids wouldn't have to ask the white man for crap. I told Charlie he was the head man in charge. It was his job to keep crap orderly round there. I told Glen he had to control his attitude. I told Tim he was in charge of customer relations. He had to make sure all the clients was 100% satisfied with our service, and he would also be in charge of bringing in new business, since he was a good hustler. In all, I told them they where extensions of me, and I was only as good as them, because they were the ones who made the shop successful by doing all the work, so instructions wasn't anything they wasn't already use to. The only difference was if anything happen to me, they would be building our business for themselves and their family.

After my little talk with them young cats you should have seen them standing there, looking like the KKK was standing in front of them. Charlie didn't say anything... he just turned and walked away. Tim came over, gave me a hug and told me he appreciated everything I ever done for him and his family. If it wasn't for me, he said, he probably would be on lock down. Glen came over after him, "Stay up. Boss. I'll see you when you finish doing what you got to do, and don't worry about the shop or Connie. We got this. Now go handle yo business, Big Homey."

As I was walking out the shop, I looked back at Charlie behind the counter. No words needed… I knew by the way he looked at me he had crap on lock, so I bounced out.

Now for the hard part… On that seemingly long drive to Morehouse to pick Connie up, I was rehearsing in my mind what I was going to say to her. I needed to tell her she wasn't going back to Detroit, and that I had to leave that night. I also needed to tell her what to do just in case I didn't make it back home. That was the hardest part. How could I tell her something like, "What you need to do in case I don't come back…" when I promised her so much, so fast because I never knew what love was until she came into my life, and was quick to grab it? This woman made me feel so alive without any constraints on my life. She knew me from the moment she laid eyes on me back in White Castle that dark, gloomy, lonely night. She knew the real Richard William Jones, not "Sweet Dick Willie Jones", the one that I was beginning to despise that night.

When Connie got into the car she did her usual thing—slid right up next to me like them white gals do riding with them red neck, confederate flag trucking White men. She gave me a kiss, looked into my eyes for a second, and just smiled.

You see, Connie always did this, thinking she was slick. She did this in order to read my eyes. She could read me like a book from the moment she looked into them. I couldn't hide whatever I was feeling from her. I may not tell her whatever it was that was bothering me, and she didn't ask, but she always knew whether it was family, friends, or something she had done. And for the most part, she would get it out of me later in her own little sly way, without even asking.

You see, Connie taught me how and when to communicate something to her, something I never experienced, because I never had anyone I trusted enough to open up my soul to. With her, my spirit was free and at peace, because I didn't feel the need to hide anything from her (but my past), and she never asked me anything about that, so there was no pressure to. Again, she knew her man.

It seemed like everything that went on in Detroit had been compartmentalized somewhere back in my brain until Sam big ass showed up. Now, I had to relive all that bull again, at least for a couple more weeks.

On that ride home, Connie and I didn't say a word to one another. We just listen to our favorite riding eight-track tape, 'The Commodores" Lionel Richie singing that song, "I'm Easy Like Sunday Morning". After that song went off, I felt Connie gently kiss me underneath my ear and whisper. "Baby, you need peace! Go back where you have to and handle your business. You need peace, baby, and I need you, Richard."

I'm not going to lie to you. I did something I had never done in my entire life. I pulled the car over on the curve and actually started crying my eyes out like I'd seen my li'l girl of a brother Derek do. I had never cried before about nothing in my whole life. It was like the Hoover Dam had busted. I held onto Connie like a child crying on his mother shoulder, and she held me back like a mother comforting her sick child.

When we made it home, Connie went in first while I sat out in the car for a few more minutes, thinking to myself, "Now I know how that sap William feel with all this crying bullcrap." That would be the first and last time for this brother! To me, that had always been a sign of weakness as a man, and I broke down like a rusty ass Oldsmobile Cutlass bumper in front my woman.

"DAMN, Richard!" I said to myself. "Get your crap together. You don't need no tears in your eyes, fella. You need blood and a clear head. So I shook that sap crap off and went into the crib to pack up so I could go pick Derek up and hit the road while we still had a good amount of day light left. My plan was to arrive into Detroit under the cover of night.

When I got into the crib Connie had my one brown raggedy suit case all packed up by the door. She gave me a kiss and said she'll see me when I get back. I picked up my suit case, turned and walked away from her without even kissing her good-bye or saying anything. I look back now and I wonder why I did that. Maybe it was after crying in front my woman like a li'l girl, I needed to regain that coldness that sheltered me up until that point. I don't know, but whatever it was, Connie didn't say a word. She just rolled with it like that day I dropped her off in front of her Grandma's in the snow.

On that ride to Mom crib, my mind snapped back into trapping mode (planning). The whom, what, and where details of my plan, you know! *The one I didn't have.*

Again, I worked the scenario from the end backwards to the beginning where I was then. Plant the book on a sucka, contact Sam and give him the mark, and get back to my woman ...simple as that in my mind.

When I got to Mom place Derek was upstairs in his room laying on his bed, looking like his eyes was about to pop out his head. They were so swollen from him crying. I told him to get his ass up and talk to me. I told Derek wasn't nothing back in Detroit but a bunch of dope dealing Negros and bad memories for both of us. Then it hit me. The light bulb popped on in my head. I know who to frame with the books... those dope boys who hung out at the shop! They didn't like Tracy. They wanted in on her action. They didn't like a chick running crap. They tried to kill my li'l brother. And most of all, I hated dope dealers ever since Mom got pinch and had to do two pennies. To me, they where the scum of the earth, so I didn't care about none of them. Hell, to me, the more of them dead would be doing the community a social service.

When we crossed over the Ohio line into Michigan you could tell you were in raggedy ass Michigan. I-75 went from smooth to pot holes rough all the way to Detroit. It was like going fifty-five up a long dirt road, they were so messed up.

When we passed Tiger Stadium, it was official to me we were in the Motor City again. My mind switched into animal mode, like that day when I got off that van on the yard at juvie (reform school) back in Minnesota.

"Let the games begin!"

All the way to Michigan from Atlanta I grudged up my hatred for drug dealers in order for me to get to the point where I needed to be to pull this setup off without my conscious getting in the way. I had to remember how much I disliked them for planting their poison on my Mom and almost killing my li'l brother. But vividly in my memory was that day when Tracy scooped (hired) me up out the detail shop— how I looked back at them, the way they looked at me, and me thinking how I would love to make the world a couple Negros better by killing all them dope dealing son-of-a-tricks. So, to me, they were the perfect ass-holes to trap (setup).

Chapter 12

Cleaning Up a Dirty World

It was round about two-thirty a.m. that Saturday morning when I dropped Derek off just outside of Highland Park on Seven Mile Road and Woodward, near Palmer Park at one of his ferry (gay) friend's house. I told him in two days I would be back to pick him up, and his ass better be ready. Until then, I would not see him or talk to him, and he wasn't to even mention my name to no one.

After dropping Derek off, I jumped back onto Woodward Avenue and headed north toward Birmingham. But soon as I crossed over the Eight Mile Road bridge, just past the State Fair Ground, I looked over to my right and noticed White Castle. It was the same one where I first met my ol' lady, and I was kind'a hungry. So I did a u-turn and made my way back to the joint.

I pulled into the parking lot about to go through the drive through, but something told me, "No. Go in, Richard". I had always had a habit of listening to my senses, especially in a situation where I had to be on guard at all times.

When my senses told me something, whatever it was usually was good for my health. So I parked my ride and went inside. When I walked into the place, it was the normal "after the club close crowd" standing in line, all decked out in their clean peacock rags, talking loud and bugging out! "Why did I come in here?" I was thinking to myself. Then something told me to look over to my left, and it was that old drunk who ran the detail shop, sitting his ass up in the corner with his head hung down, looking like he had been drinking all night.

When I walked over to him and tapped his ass on the shoulder; that son-of-a-switch turned and jump like he seen Jesus himself. "Sweet Dick Willie Jones!" that oil head yelled out! Everyone in the place got quiet and looked at me like Moses himself had stepped into the joint. I looked over to them and gave a look back that must have said what tens of thousands of words couldn't, because they all turned back around as quickly as they turned to see.

I told the old boy I needed to talk to him outside. He got up with no questions, and we both went out to my ride to talk. I didn't say a word. I looked at him and his ass started shaking like Don Knotts again, reaching inside his jacket pocket for his bottle. He took it out and took a long swig from the neck, and then started singing like Diana Ross on cocaine.

He started out by telling me about what happen to Tracy—how the broad got too big for her lace panties trying to run a man hustle; how that so-and-so thought she couldn't be touched, sitting her ass up in that high rise in Southfield with them Jews, but they got to her. He starts bragging about how he got the shop, and now that so-and-so can't tell him what to do anymo. I wanted to stop him right then, but something told me to keep letting that bastard talk. Then he said through all that mumbling crap, "I know that fag did something with them books. Maybe gave it to one of his sissy boy (gay) friends."

"Holy Crap!" I said to myself. Then I turned to his ass and told him to get out my car. At the same time as I was reaching over his ass to open his door to push his drunken tail out my ride, I started the engine and burned rubber out of White Castle parking lot like Richard Pryor when that fire jumped on his ass. I had to get to Derek quick. This crap was a setup. Whoever iced (killed) Derek punk boy friend must think he gave them books to my li'l brother. The stuff just kept getting crazier fast!

When I got to the spot where I drop Derek off at the front door was kicked in, and the spot was wrecked like a tornado had ran through it. "Oh, DAMN!" I said to myself. They had my li'l brother, and for once I couldn't think of what the hell to do. I was mad, and I'm not going to lie, I was *afraid* too. I can take someone messing with me, but my family is another level, especially my li'l brother. The realization of me saying all those times, "I would die for my family and Connie" was telling me to stop saying that, because we speak our world into existence, so I guess it was true. So at that point, I was scared, but prepared to die to get my li'l brother back.

I needed to know who had my li'l brother and the only person I could think of was that drunken bastard I left back up at White Castle. But by the time I got back up there his ass, as expected, was gone. I didn't trip... I knew where he could be found first thing Monday morning. My only hope was that Derek would still be alive.

"Really, what can I do now?" I repeated to myself. Detroit was a big city. I couldn't run all over it like a chicken with my head cut off looking for him, tipping whoever off. So I decided to head to Birmingham and get me a room at the Holiday Inn off Woodward.

I couldn't sleep. All night I laid on the bed with my cloths on listening to WJZZ 105.9 thinking of my next move. Finally, as day was about to break, I fell asleep for what seemed like twenty-four hours, but it was only two hours before my nerves awaken me. Or maybe it was an angel or something. I can't recall now.

On that drive to the Eastside of Detroit where the detail shop was located, I was getting this feeling like it wasn't going to be a good day. As I pulled into the parking lot of the shop, that feeling got even stronger. There were no cars up there, like the place was closed. But the "Open for Business" sign was showing. I turned off the engine and just sat there for a few seconds. I don't know... as I look back now, maybe I was making peace with my Maker for all the things I had ever done up to that point, and, crazy as it sounds, I turned over any fear in my heart to him. It was time for me to walk into that lion's den with my pork chop draws on, dripping blood from the meat.

3

When I walked into the shop it was like I had stepped into hell and was greeted by the Devil himself. It was Sam's big ass. Standing behind the counter with that messed up grin on his face saying to me, "What's up, Li'l Nigga?" I didn't flinch or trip. I just told his big ass my li'l brother better be good. Sam replied, "That li'l fag cool right now, but if you don't give up them books you won't have to worry about that li'l sissy no mo', cause after I put some hurt on you I'm going to shove my Johnson so far up that li'l ferry, his tonsils gone fall out! Then I'm a give him to this John trick back in da Twin (Minnesota) to trick out."

I started seeing Daddy black ass when he said that. Before he could get trick out his mouth I was on his big ass like a cheetah on a big ass wilderbeast. I always knew me and Sam would come to blows eventually. We fought until we both got tired. I can't say I took a ass whipping, but he can't say he whipped my ass, either. I wasn't the biggest cat, but I wasn't the weakest either, and by the time the body blows stopped, he knew he had stepped into a li'l nigga that he seriously under-estimated.

When I look back now, it scares me to think of how I just reacted when Sam made the comment about my li'l brother; I guess the same way I reacted when Daddy blew that bullcrap out his mouth. Sam was use to guns and knives taking cats out like a snapper. He hadn't been challenged physically in a fight probably in a long time, so his hand game wasn't the sharpest. I guess when you're as big as him, didn't nobody jump too quick to challenge you to a fight. That's why I laughed when I saw on BET news that boy knocking Suge Knight out some time ago... Lol.

"Where is my brother, Sam?" I said to him in a calm, cool voice.

"Your brother back there. li'l nigga (pointing to the back of the shop where the supplies where kept)." When I opened that door and seen Derek tied up in that chair with blood running down the side of his mouth and forehead, I turn back to Sam big ass (who was still sitting on the floor wiping blood off the side of his mouth). I dashed toward his big ass and kicked the crap out of him dead to the side of his head in the temple, knocking him straight out. I turned back toward Derek, ran to him and un-tied him. Thank God he was still breathing, or Sam big ass would have woke up dead, fa sho.

I took Derek out to my car and made sure he was safely in. Then I reached under the driver side dashboard and pulled out Tracy books and stared at them for a few seconds before I walked back into the shop.

I woke Sam big ass up, and the first thing that big nigga said was, "Ain't nobody ever knocked me out before, or even ever tried to challenge me in a fight, and yo' li'l ass did all that!" Then he gave that messed up laugh and commented, "You never gave me a chance to ready myself, li'l nigga, before you jumped me, you know or I would have whipped you li'l ass!" Then he reached out to give me a pound (shake my hand) but I didn't extend mine back. I told him forget all that, and threw Tracy's funky ass books on his lap. I told him all I want is for me and my family to be left alone. Those books and whatever content they contain don't mean a damn thing to me or my family, and him and whoever else can take them and shove them up their asses for all I care. Just leave us alone.

Sam looked up at me and shook his head in agreement. He asked me where I found the books. I told him it didn't matter... he had them, so they where his problem now. I couldn't give a damn what he did with them.

As I was about to walk out the door Sam called to me. "Hey li'l Nigga..." I didn't even turn around, I just paused. "Take care yourself." I didn't say a word in return to him. I continued out the door to my car to check on my li'l brother and get out of that raggedy hell hole of a city fast as I could.

On the long drive back to Atlanta; Derek and I didn't talk at all. As bad as I wanted to know what he was thinking, I couldn't bring myself to ask him his thoughts because it would have just killed me if he had said something about some gay crap. So I left him inside his own head all the way back to our new home in Atlanta.

When we got to mom place Derek gave me a big hug, and said "Thanks, R.J." Derek also told me all his life he knew who has always protected him, and that he was sorry he didn't turn out to be the man I wanted him to be. I told Derek it didn't matter; he is my brother no matter what type of lifestyle he chooses to live, and as long as there's life in my body, I would be there for him. Then I told him to get out my car with a rare smile on my face.

As I was backing out Mom's driveway, something told me to pause and look to the left at Mrs. Clara house. Somehow, I just felt she was sitting on that dark screen porch, puffing on her pipe, smiling at me, letting me know that the wata has return to calm now, Willow Mae Jones boy. I gave a smile back to her then headed for home.

I couldn't wait to see Connie. I must have driven a hundred miles per hour to our place. When I stepped into the door I could smell the aroma of that sweet apple cinnamon incense she loves. I opened the door to find my beautiful woman sleeping soundly on my side of the bed, in one of my tee shirts and draws. I sat on the end of the bed, ran the back of my hand lightly across her forehead and stared for what seemed like eternity at her. When she awakened to see me, she jumped up and almost squeezed every bit of love I had in me out. Now mind you, my body was still sore as hell from that battle with Sam sixteen hours before, compounded by a hell of a drive, so her hug was like joy and pain to my mind, body, and soul. I told my sweet lady it finally was over.

LETTING GO

If we contemplate desires and listen to them, we are actually no longer attaching to them; we are just allowing them to be the way they are. Then we come to the realization that the origin of suffering, desire, can be laid aside and let go of.

Epilog

I met Richard Jones by accident, you could say. One day on the Eastside of Detroit visiting my partner Andre, we walked up the street to a lady friend of his' house. When we walked into the house, I could see this old dude chilling in the kitchen with the gal's mom that Andre came to see. Well, actually the old broad was doing all the talking while the ol' dude just sat there chilling, listening.

While Dre and his friend went into another room to kick it, I sat on the end of a couch that was right next to the doorway to the kitchen.

The old man was strikingly interesting looking to me, and his demeanor was laid back and reserved. You could tell he wasn't a man of many words, as the lady continued to run off at the mouth about what sounded like the old days. Before I could turn my head to pretend I wasn't eavesdropping, the old dude had turned to me, catching me dead in my eyes. It was a cold look, as it froze me in my seat. The only thing I could do was say, "How ya'll doing?" He nodded without saying a word, and then turned his attention back to the old woman.

****

When Dre and his lady friend came out from the other room, we all went onto the front porch. I ask the girl who was the old cat in the kitchen kicking it with her old girl. She told me the woman was her grandma, and he was her best friend's husband up visiting from Atlanta. His wife had died a month earlier, so he came up to get some things her grandma had been keeping for her. She also said her Grandma never talked much about them, but she had found a bunch of letters in their basement one night from his wife written to her Grandma, and they where sooo beautifully written, like something from a fairy tale about him and her.

I don't know what it was, but something was telling me I needed to talk to the old dude. I went back into the house, straight to the kitchen, and introduced myself to them.

Talking about awkward moments... this was one for me. I looked him straight in his eyes and told him something in my spirit was telling me I needed to listen to him. He looked back at me with the coldest eyes I had ever seen my life. I felt so much pain, fear and sadness from his eyes, but I also sensed a strong sense of strength, as well.

He motioned for me to sit down. Without saying anything to me, I knew he wanted me to tell him something about myself. I told him I was born in Louisiana, moved to Minnesota when I was in fifth grade, then to Flint, Michigan in my last month of the fifth, and finally to Pontiac, Michigan, for my sixth grade.

He stopped me and asked why I moved around so much. I told him my Mom was sort of a nomad when I was growing up, moving from one place to another in the blink of an eye, hauling my brother and me along the way.

He suddenly stopped me again. He told me he had a story to tell me, and what I did with it was no matter to him. I asked him "Why me?" His response—"Why not you, boy?"

For that next week I spent hours with Mr. Jones just listening to his story. I even drove him over to Windsor, Canada, and we sat on a bench on the shore of the Detroit River talking, walking, and eating ice cream cones, looking back over the river at the Detroit side while listening to his story.

****

For years I didn't know what to do with it. Well, actually I forgot all about it. I didn't decide to write this book until about three months ago while back in Detroit visiting a lady friend I use to kick it with. When I ran into the chick my boy Dre was hollering at in Church's Chicken on the corner of Seven mile and Gratiot. She told me the old dude had passed away a couple of months prior down in Atlanta. She said she took her grandma to the funeral, and it was so sad but beautiful. You could tell he was a loner because it wasn't many folks at his funeral, but there was a beautiful photo of him and Connie when they were younger, and her grandma read one of Connie's letters to him as he laid there peacefully in his casket. My grandma also said he looked like he finally found peace in this Dirty World.

Connie was the only woman he had ever loved. His love for her was deeper than his love for his own mother. Connie had been the only pure, clean ray of inspiration for him in this dirty world, and without her, my grandma said she was surprised he lived without her as long as he did.

After talking with her, his story started haunting me like a ghost trying to be released so it could travel onto its final resting place.

I finally decided to sit down and start writing Mr. Jones' story. Although I'm definitely not a writer, it was extremely important that I bring closure to his story.

Some will read this story and believe it's fiction or fairy tale, but I assure you it's what Mr. Jones told me, except the names have been changed. Though I only knew him briefly, no other person has had such a profound impact on my life as he did. I found out parts of my life weren't that far off from his. I guess that's probably why our paths crossed in this life.

I learned from Mr. Jones that we don't get an opportunity to choose what type of lifestyle we're born into, but we do have a choice on the type of lifestyle we will live. He told me one thing I should always remain watchful of, and it is:

"Life will always come full circle if you're not mindful of the present, in this Dirty World".

Made in the USA
Lexington, KY
08 September 2010